MODERN   FOREIGN   EXCHANGE

THE MACMILLAN COMPANY
NEW YORK · BOSTON · CHICAGO · DALLAS
ATLANTA · SAN FRANCISCO

MACMILLAN & CO., Limited
LONDON · BOMBAY · CALCUTTA
MELBOURNE

THE MACMILLAN COMPANY
OF CANADA, Limited
TORONTO

MODERN FOREIGN EXCHANGE

EXCHANGE

AN ELEMENTARY TREATISE
FOR THE LAY READER

BY

FRANKLIN ESCHER

1933

THE MACMILLAN COMPANY : NEW YORK

Set up and electrotyped. Published November, 1932. Reprinted
May, July, 1933.

PRINTED IN THE UNITED STATES OF AMERICA
NORWOOD PRESS LINOTYPE, INC.
NORWOOD, MASS., U.S.A.

INTRODUCTION

IN matters financial as well as political, America's period of splendid isolation has become definitely a thing of the past. Formerly of purely academic interest, the condition of the foreign money markets, the position of the foreign exchanges and the in-and-out movement of gold have come to have for us a very real and positive concern. No longer as was formerly the case does the term "foreign exchange" connote a specialized department of banking, of interest only to bankers and to exporters and importers of merchandise. Knowledge of the conditions reflected in the movement of the foreign exchanges has today become an indispensable factor in the formation of any true judgment of the financial picture as a whole.

Yet to many people on matters financial otherwise well informed, the whole subject of exchange and the exchanges remains an unfathomable mystery. They see the financial pages of the newspapers they read devoted to a greater and greater extent to discussion of questions of inter-country finance; yet these discussions they pass by as being beyond their understanding. They realize in a vague way that these things must have come to possess a good deal of importance to have so much attention paid to them; yet they dismiss the whole matter from consideration on the ground that it is all beyond them. Some day they feel, perhaps, some one will make an exposition of these things which they will be able to comprehend and which will provide them with the knowledge necessary for an understanding of the subject. Till then—well, if they don't understand all this business about foreign exchange they don't, and that is all there is to it.

It was for the purpose of providing this much needed explanation of what to many people is a difficult subject that the writing of this book was undertaken.

Essentially, "Modern Foreign Exchange" will be found a discussion of principles. Examples drawn from the actual post war experience of the exchange markets have, it is true, been freely used, but always in elucidation of a principle previously laid down. That, indeed, has been the author's scheme—first to present the principles which underlie the action of exchange and the exchange markets and then, by references to specific occurrences, to illustrate their actual operation. The bringing of these references to current events into a work of this kind was, it was soon enough found, a touchy business and one fraught with the danger of being led off on to controversial ground. Constantly, in the discussion of such events for instance as the international "run" on the London banks in the summer of 1931 and the subsequent fight to save the pound, the writer had to keep before him the rigid necessity of presenting these matters in the expository rather than the argumentative form.

With what degree of success the reader will have for himself to judge.

A very definite scheme, it will further be found, has been followed in the presentation of the material contained in "Modern Foreign Exchange." The opening chapters, for example, even at the risk of giving the entire work too academic a tone, have been deliberately devoted to a more or less theoretical discussion of the why and wherefore of the exchanges, of what brings them into existence, of what makes exchange rates rise and fall. That necessary groundwork having been laid, the discussion proceeds naturally to the far more practical subject of the interrelation of exchange rates, to their influence on inter-country movements of gold, and, finally, to a rather intimate description of the world's principal foreign exchange markets and the various operations carried on by the foreign exchange bankers. The long-suffering reader being presumed now to have been equipped with a working knowledge of the subject, the discussion is extended to what may be called the abnormal influences in today's exchange markets—to the conditions created by the huge inter-governmental borrowings of recent years and the subsequent control sought to be exerted upon the exchange markets by the great governmental banks. Finally, with the general picture thus drawn, the gold standard is broadly considered, particular emphasis being given to the question of the relationship of gold-standard and non-gold-standard using countries.

The entire plan, in other words, has been to lead

logically from a preliminary theoretical discussion through to the practical aspects of the subject, and, so, on to those immensely important current developments in the exchange market by which the situation is being so profoundly affected.

In no sense is "Modern Foreign Exchange" a manual of foreign exchange practice. Conspicuously lacking will be found the tables, the computations, the forms, which, to the author's way of thinking at least, serve only to confuse the lay reader. Constantly in the preparation of this book he has had in mind the reader not so much interested in the intricacies of foreign exchange practice as in the gaining of a clear perspective of the subject as a whole.

If then in the attainment of this object there shall have been any measure of success, if through the preparation of this treatise there shall have been contributed anything toward a better and clearer understanding of those vitally important principles governing the financial intercourse between ourselves and the outside world, the author will consider his labor to have been well repaid.

CONTENTS

MODERN   FOREIGN   EXCHANGE

CHAPTER I

INTER–COUNTRY DEBITS AND CREDITS

In every country having important financial relationships with the outside world there are at all times people who owe money to people in other countries and other people to whom money is owed from abroad. Originating from a variety of causes, this condition of debts to and claims upon people located in foreign countries will always and at all times be found in every important financial center.

As between any two given points, if these debts and claims were exactly equal, there would be no such thing as a "rate of exchange." The parties at one point having claims upon the other would simply sell their claims to those having payments to make abroad and all existing indebtedness between the two markets would thus be settled without the transfer of any funds whatever. He owes me and you owe him; pay me direct and leave him out of it entirely—that is the way in which it would work.

Unfortunately, however, as between any two markets, the relative indebtedness never *is* equal. Not only in actual practice will it be found that the sum total which one market owes is greater than that owed by the other, but there will be also found a wide variation in the time in which payment has to be made. New York might by some odd chance at some

given moment happen to owe London the same amount
as it was owed by London; but never, under any possible circumstances, could it be the case that payment
of these debts all had to be made at the same time.
The bulk of inter-country claims, be it remembered,
are claims to receive money not at once but over the
course of several weeks or even several months. As
between two markets, one might actually owe very
much more than the other and yet if the debts of the
market owing the larger amount were not payable for
several months while those of the other happened
to be payable on demand, the latter market might
conceivably be hard put to it to meet its obligations.

Relative Indebtedness

Fundamentally, it will thus be seen, it is this in-
equality of debts and claims which is what is responsible for there being a "rate of exchange" and
for the fact that this rate rises and falls. The fact, it
is true, that the debts and claims referred to are expressed in different currencies—that New York, for
example, may be owed in dollars and may owe in
pounds sterling—has something to do with it; but,
fundamentally, it is not a matter of currency at all,
but of demand and supply. The case of two markets
having an identical currency, New York and Montreal
for example, shows this very clearly. Does the fact
that both markets use the same currency prevent the
dollar payable in Montreal (Canadian currency) from
selling at a premium or a discount as compared with
the dollar payable in New York? Not in the least.
What counts is the extent of the demand for dollars

payable in Montreal by those who have payments to make at that point as against the supply of dollars payable in Montreal by those who have claims there which they are entitled to sell.

For purposes of illustration, the United States, we will say, is heavily indebted to France and the time has come when large payments have to be made. If, now, France owes us little, in other words if there are few here with claims on Paris which they are in a position to sell to those who have to make payments in Paris, it is very evident that there will be sharp competition for those claims and that buyers will be willing to pay a substantial premium to get them. Here again, we see, it is not because the claims happen to be payable in francs or in any foreign currency whatsoever that they are in such demand. What makes them so valuable is that they happen to be claims for money at a point where heavy payments have to be made. What gives the owner a chance to sell them at a high price is the fact of his having a given sum already at a point where it is required by another.

Since then it is this question of the debts and claims of countries which is the primary influence on the rate of exchange between them, it is evident that in any study of the exchanges a definite comprehension of this matter of relative indebtedness is of the first importance. When and only when this question, which underlies the whole theory of foreign exchange, is clearly in mind and we have a definite understanding of the various ways in which countries come to owe each other money, can we satisfactorily proceed to

consider the form taken by this indebtedness when the
time of payment arrives and the bill of exchange
takes the place of the floating debt. Later, the discussion will lead logically to the bill of exchange itself, to its nature, to its form, to the various things
which determine its current price.

Origin of Debts and Claims

What then are the main circumstances which bring
into existence the inter-country debts and claims
above referred to?

(1) First and most important of these, without
doubt, is the shipment of merchandise from one country to another. A firm in New Orleans, we will say,
makes a sale of cotton to a mill in Liverpool, England. Instantly there comes into existence a claim for
a certain number of dollars by the seller in America
upon the buyer in England. Later, when the cotton
has been fabricated and sold perhaps by the Liverpool
mill to a distributor of cotton goods in Paris, there is
originated a claim for a certain number of pounds
sterling by the seller in England upon the buyer in
France. And so it goes. All the time merchandise of
one sort or another is being sold by parties in one
country to parties in another country; and, as a result
of these sales, inter-country money claims are all the
time being brought into existence. (With the *method*
by which these claims are settled we are not at present
concerned; what we have first to consider are the
various circumstances under which they originate.)

A time when shipments of merchandise are running

strongly from one country "A" to another "B," it is thus to be noted, will naturally be a time when there will be created large claims by the merchants of "A" upon the merchants of "B."

(2) Shipments of securities, of course, have exactly the same effect toward creating these inter-country claims of the seller upon the buyer as have shipments of merchandise. Because of the large number of pounds sterling which can be bought with the dollar proceeds or for any other cause, London, we will say, is at some given time selling her holdings of American securities freely on the New York Stock Exchange. Immediately, then, there come into existence claims by the sellers in London upon the buyers in New York. Claims usually for substantial amounts, it is important to note, by reason of the fact that international selling movements of securities, when they once begin, are likely to run into volume. Nothing in the way of merchandise shipments, not even for example the cotton shipments from the U. S. A. which always run in such large amount in the early autumn, have an effect comparable, in the way of creating claims upon the buyers, to that arising from these concentrated inter-country security-selling movements.

Flotation of bond issues by one country in another, have an effect even stronger. Further along, of course, the bonds will come due and set the current of claims running the other way; but, during the time that the bonds are originally being sold, very large money claims upon the country where the bonds are being placed will inevitably be established.

(3) This matter of the securities of one country held by another naturally suggests a further source of inter-country claims, that arising from the interest and dividends which must continually be sent to the holders of such securities. Chile, for example, or Brazil, may have sold their bonds in the United States and for the time being thus have established large claims for dollars on New York; but, almost immediately, there is set up a counter claim (though of course in much lesser amount) for the interest on these bonds which the borrowing country must pay. Especially, as in the case of these South American bonds where the interest runs as high as seven or eight percent, these interest claims constitute a formidable item. In the case of a bond bearing an eight percent coupon, it is evident, there is developed during the very first year of the life of the loan a claim upon the borrowing country amounting to no less than one-twelfth of the principal amount. And where, in addition to the interest, there is a sinking-fund provision, the claim is correspondingly that much more.

(4) It is, however, by no means only through the export of goods or securities that debts and claims are created. Services rendered by people in one country to people in another have quite the same effect. Maritime nations, for example, like England or Sweden or Norway, in whose ships a substantial portion of the world's commerce is carried, are constantly accumulating freight-charge claims upon the countries to whom these services are being rendered. Similarly with regard to insurance or banking service.

England, for example, so far as international trade is concerned, for years and years was—and to a surprising extent still is—the world's banker. Which means, of course, that for the commissions arising from their services in financing the export and import business of other countries, British bankers have at all times substantial claims upon exporters and importers in those countries.

(5) In the establishment of international money claims a further important part, again, is played by the expenditures of tourists and of those resident in foreign countries. Take for example the case of the American colony in Paris. Here, year in and year out, very large amounts of money are being spent, all of which must be drawn from the United States. Avoiding, as for the moment we must continue to avoid, any description of *how* inter-country transfers of money are actually made, it must nevertheless even at this early stage in the discussion be plain that when an American resident in Paris expends money he must, by that very act, be passing along to somebody or other a claim upon his bankers in the States. Somehow and in some way, it is evident, the funds must be transferred from America to Paris or wherever it is that they are being spent.

In the case of a rich country like this with many of its wealthy citizens living abroad a great part of the time and with thousands upon thousands of others crossing the water each year for the purpose of touring in foreign countries, it is plain that the claims upon us arising from the expenditures of our expatriates, permanent and temporary, must in the aggregate run into a very large sum.

(6) For the sake of complete and orderly presentation, even at the risk of running a little ahead of our subject, one other source of inter-country claims must be mentioned. Where, as frequently happens in the case of countries having close financial relationships, the rate of interest happens to be ruling temporarily higher in one country than the other, short-term inter-country loans (60 days to 6 months) are all the time being made between bankers in order to profit from this condition. In order to take advantage of a higher loaning rate prevailing in country "A," we will say, banks and bankers in country "B" transfer to country "A" a portion of the mobile funds they have available for loaning. What is the effect? To set up a claim by the borrower upon the lender, of course, at the time the loan is made; but later, when the loan comes due, to reverse the process and to set up a claim by the lender upon the borrower, now under the necessity of returning the funds. This, then, all the time where the financial relationship between two countries is at all close, is going on: Short-term loans setting up claims, at the time they are made, by one market on another; and these claims, as the loans come due, being reversed in direction.

(7) Having considered, in the foregoing, the principal circumstances which give rise to money claims by individuals and groups in one country upon individuals and groups in another, we have now to con-

sider that other and vastly important class of claims existing directly between governments. These we shall find to consist of (a) the repayment of temporary loans made directly by one government to another during and just after the Great War, and (b) those vexed inter-government payments commonly known as "Reparations."

Taking this question of "Reparations" first, it is plain that a work of this kind is no place for discussion of the right or wrong of what was "settled" by the Treaty of Versailles or of the successive modifications thereof by which there has been determined the amount which Germany is at present presumed to owe. Stating the matter in its simplest terms, the Government of Germany (*not* individuals or groups of individuals in Germany) is obligated to pay annually to the Governments of France and England and others of the Allies, certain specified amounts in francs, pounds sterling and other currencies. How the German Government is to provide itself with these funds for transmission abroad—what means it is to employ, in other words, for providing itself with the necessary funds—is left to the German Government. Theoretically at least, actually as a matter of fact, as long as the payments are maintained as per schedule, the various creditor governments are concerned only that at a specified time and a specified place the money is to be to them paid in hand.

With regard to the claims mentioned above, it is well to note at this time, the United States is in no way concerned except as their payment or non-payment affects the ability of the claimants to discharge their various financial obligations to the U. S. A. We ourselves having exacted no "Reparations," have no direct claims on the German Government or the people of Germany. If it is of any interest to us one way or the other whether France and England and the others are able to collect from Germany, that is solely because of their contention that unless they *are* able to collect on their claims, it is impossible for them to pay the interest, let alone the principal, on what they owe the United States.

That brings us down to the other class of these inter-governmental claims, those of the Government of the United States upon the Governments of England, France and the rest of the Allies. Whatever may have been the wisdom and the necessity for lending out these billions of dollars, the loans *were* made, and unless or until they are cancelled, they constitute a direct claim on the part of the U. S. Government upon these others. Not, it must be clearly understood, upon individuals or groups of individuals in England or France or the other countries which borrowed from us, but upon the governments of these countries.

To avoid any possibility of misunderstanding it may be well here to state, even at the risk of redundancy, that these inter-governmental loans we are speaking about are entirely separate from and have nothing whatever to do with, the government bond issues sold in this country by England, France and the others of the Allies. What we are speaking of now are the temporary loans which were made by the U. S. Government first during the course of the War in order to make it possible for the Allies to buy munitions and war supplies; and, secondly, just after the War in order to make possible the reconstruction of the devastated areas.

Whatever may have been the method of reimbursement envisaged either by borrower or lender at the time these loans were made, it is a fact that with regard to a large part of this debt, even now, fourteen years after the end of the War, it has never been determined in what amount or even in what form repayment is to be made. The claims stand, of course, but the question as to how and when and even whether they are to be discharged has not yet been actually settled.

"Balance of Trade"

Having considered in the foregoing the various circumstances which give rise to inter-country debts and claims, we are now in a position to examine the question of the mutual indebtedness between any two countries or, as it is more generally known, the "balance of trade."

It will be very evident at the outset that the striking of a financial balance between two countries is a very different proposition from the striking of a balance between, let us say, two corporations. In the latter instance the debits and credits are clearly defined, so-and-so-much bought from and so-and-so-much sold to. In the former, that is very far from being the case. The debits and credits, we have seen, originate from a large variety of causes, and the time of settlement may or may not have been definitely fixed. Also, there is the fact that while the figures on some of these inter-country operations are available (the figures on mer-chandise exports and imports, for example), on others they are not. Who, for instance, is in a position to say what in any given year we owe the rest of the world by reason of American tourists' expenditures abroad; or, again, what our bill may be for premiums on in-surance written here by European insurance com-panies? Yet, if any true "balance" is to be struck be-tween ourselves and any other country, each and every one of these items must be fully taken into account.

This question, then, of the "balance of trade" is a very deceptive thing; there is a great deal more to it, evidently, than just the difference between a country's exports and a country's imports. What is often un-thinkingly referred to as an "adverse" trade balance or an "unfavorable" trade balance may, upon closer examination, turn out to be quite the reverse. On straight merchandise export and import transactions, let us say, some country in some given year is owed by another country the sum of one hundred millions. But suppose now that this apparently "creditor" country actually owes the other country fifty million on ac-count of expenditures by its tourists or its citizens resident abroad, twenty million for insurance and freight services, and perhaps still another fifty for securities purchased and imported during the year: Where, now, is the formerly apparently "favorable" balance of one hundred million? Metamorphosed, it is apparent, into an "unfavorable" balance of twenty million.

Is there not then, it may at this point well be asked, any relation between these various items of debit and credit—are there countries, for example, which habitually export much more merchandise than they import and yet which have large additional sums owing them for securities sold abroad, for freight and other services rendered to foreign countries, etc., etc.? The answer is, very simply, that the "sweet reasonableness" of the situation is that no one country can or ever does remain in the position of a habitual creditor of all the others. A country rich in natural resources and regularly a creditor on merchandise account is certain, on account of its accumulating wealth, to be a buyer rather than a seller of securities. Again, a country rich enough regularly to import more merchandise than it exports (Great Britain, for example) is bound to have an accumulated surplus of wealth invested in foreign countries the return on which goes far to offset the "unfavorable" balance on purely merchandise account. If, in other words, we find some country year after year in the same position with regard to its transactions in merchandise with the rest of the world, that is so and only so because of its other foreign financial relationships— because it habitually exports or imports securities or services, because it owes or is owed on account of citizens' expenditures abroad, etc., etc. These things are all closely interconnected and exert the strongest kind of an influence one upon the other.

With regard to this matter of the striking of a true "trade balance" between two countries, it yet remains to be pointed out that the items which go to make up such a balance at any given time are limited to those debits which are *currently* due and payable. They do not, in other words, include those debits which by common consent are held in abeyance for a long term of years, the bonds of one country, for example, held in another. An enormous sum, no doubt, is owed by the United States to Great Britain on account of the mass of American bonds owned in England; but, except for the interest on these securities, this long-term debt figures little if at all in the determination of what is the true "balance of trade." That, as we have seen, is determined entirely by current debits the time for the settlement of which has actually arrived.

With the above picture before us of what actually goes to make up the financial balance between two countries, we shall be less prone, perhaps, to jump to the conclusion that because the visible exports of a country exceed its imports its true trade balance is necessarily "favorable"; nor yet, because its imports may exceed its exports, to conclude that its balance is necessarily "adverse." An important consideration this, in these days of heavy inter-governmental debts and of searching inquiry into the physical ability of various governments to make the payments to which they are obligated.

Attempt has been made in the foregoing paragraphs to outline the main considerations responsible for the coming into existence of inter-country debts and claims. By that discussion, necessarily of a more or less theoretical nature, we shall perhaps have been brought into a position to examine these debts and claims in their more practical aspect—that is to say, to look into their influence on day-to-day markets and to study the question of the physical methods by which their settlement is actually effected. Let us proceed then to discussion, in the next chapter, of the way in which a man in one country who owes money in another discharges his debt, and of how the man who is owed gets paid.

CHAPTER II

THE BILL OF EXCHANGE

IN what way, we have now to consider, is the settlement of these inter-country claims we have been discussing actually effected? All over the world, we have seen, there are people who owe money in America, and in America there are people who owe money all over the world. To bring the matter down to one specific case, how does the man in New York, for instance, who has sold the cotton to the man in London, get paid?

What the seller in New York wants, of course, is dollars, either an order on some New York bank (a check or draft) for the number of dollars he is entitled to receive; or, failing that, the right himself to draw a draft on the buyer or the buyer's bank, which draft he (the cotton seller) can readily convert into dollars. This principle then, we must bear firmly in mind, that there are *two* ways in which the creditor can get paid: (1) The debtor abroad can either go to his home bank and buy from it a draft on its New York correspondent for the requisite number of dollars, which he will then send to the man to whom he owes the money; or (2) The debtor abroad can instruct the creditor here to draw a draft either directly on him or on some bank in New York or London designated by him. If the draft is to be made on the

16

shipper or on an English bank it will, of course, be drawn in pounds sterling; if on a bank in New York, in dollars.

From the standpoint of the creditor, in this case the American shipper of the cotton, which method of payment is most advantageous? The method, obviously, by which he himself draws a draft on a New York bank in dollars, collects the money which is due him, and is out of the transaction. Next to that, the method by which he draws a sterling draft on the buyer abroad or on his bank, sells the draft in the New York foreign exchange market for dollars, and thus gets his money at once. Least attractive is the method by which, after he has shipped the goods, he has to wait a week or ten days until a draft drawn on New York in dollars is sent to him from the other side. Of some influence, thus, in fixing the price at which the goods are to be sold, is the method of payment arranged between the buyer and the seller. "Payment by dollar credit in New York"—nothing, of course, is as satisfactory to the seller or as conducive to his quoting the best possible price on the goods.

What, besides this, determines the method by which payment for the goods is to be arranged? Mainly, it may be said, the part of the world in which the buyer is located and the scope and character of the financial market in which he does his financing. If, for instance, the buyer is located in some Central or South American center with a fluctuating currency and a tenuous relationship to the New York money market, it is very plain that the American exporter is not going to be satisfied to be told to draw a foreign currency draft which may have to be sold at a heavy discount and which may, indeed, not be salable at all. If, on the other hand, the buyer is located in some country like England or France and desires that payment be effected by the shipper drawing on him in sterling or in francs, that arrangement is likely to be considered entirely satisfactory. What we find then, as a practical matter, with regard to this question of the method of payment, is that where the shipment is being made to a country with a strongly established financial market, payment by draft on the buyer or the buyer's bank is the usual thing; whereas, in the case of shipments to lesser points, payment is more apt to be made by means of a dollar credit established by the buyer with some New York bank.

Some forms of indebtedness are customarily settled the first way, some by the second. So far as the influence on the foreign exchanges is concerned, the effect, as we shall presently see, is exactly the same in the one case as in the other. The mechanics of the thing is simplicity itself. The conditions, however, which make possible the two forms of settlement are something to which we shall find it worth while to give a little further thought.

Buyers and Sellers

How is it, in the first place, it may well be asked, that the maker of the sterling draft can always find some one who will take it off his hands and give him dollars for it? How is it, in the second place, that the buyer of the cotton abroad can always find some one willing to sell him a draft on New York drawn in dollars?

The answer to the first question, very simply, is that just as there are people in New York with money claims upon people in London (which claims are to be settled by drawing drafts on London) so there are other people in New York who owe money in London (which debts are to be discharged through the sending to London of sterling drafts). In other words, just as there is all the time being created a supply of sterling drafts so there is all the time being created a demand for sterling drafts.

The answer to the second question is, essentially, the same. If in London there are all the time people under the necessity of sending dollar drafts to people in New York to whom they owe money, there are also others continually drawing dollar drafts on people in New York upon whom they have claims.

What then we see continuously going on in this business of foreign exchange is the selling of claims to receive money at some given point to parties who have debts to discharge at that same point. "A" in London has a claim on some one in New York for a thousand dollars. "B" in London owes somebody in New York a thousand dollars. If "A" in London sells his claim to "B" in London and "B" passes his claim along to the party in New York to whom he owes the money, the whole transaction, it is plain, will have been completed with a minimum amount of trouble.

In effect that is exactly what happens, but there is a further angle to the matter of just how it happens which must be appreciated if we are clearly to understand this business of the buying and selling of drafts on foreign countries. Granted that at every important financial center like London or New York there are people who have drafts to buy and other people who have drafts to sell, it is self-evident that the man in London, for instance, who has a draft on some New York mercantile house for, say, $1369.59 to sell, is not very probably going to find somebody looking for just that kind of draft and for exactly that amount. The claim in question on New York for approximately thirteen hundred dollars may be there, and someone may want to make a remittance to New York for an amount somewhere around thirteen hundred dollars; but, even so, it must be plain, a direct transaction between the two parties is hardly a possible solution of the matter. In some way, through some intermediary, the claim on New York must be made available to the party in need of purchasing such a claim.

The Foreign Exchange Banker

Just here is where the foreign exchange banker comes into the picture. Maintaining balances with correspondent banks in important financial centers all over the world, he stands ready at any time to buy drafts from anyone who has drafts to sell or to sell drafts to anyone who wishes to buy. Never, however, remember, does the foreign exchange banker act in the capacity of a *broker*—the actual drafts which he purchases he never resells. These, as soon as he buys them, he sends to his correspondent bank in the foreign city on which they are drawn with instructions that they be credited to his account. Thus when some one comes along and wants to buy a draft on that particular city, the banker is in a position to sell it to him. *His own draft,* observe, drawn upon a balance built up and maintained by his purchases of the drafts of various kinds and amounts which are continually being offered him.

Through the medium of the foreign exchange banker, it will thus be seen, it not only becomes possible for the man having a legitimate draft of any kind or amount to dispose of it for cash, but it becomes possible, as well, to buy any kind of a draft for any given amount on any particular city. The foreign exchange banker's deposit account with his correspondent abroad may thus be regarded as a kind of clearing house for debts and claims. Into his account go the drafts he buys—drafts of all sizes and kinds; drafts drawn on bankers, merchants and individuals; drafts drawn payable at sight and anywhere up to four months after sight. Out of his account come the drafts he sells—drafts of exactly the kind and amount required by his customers. A sort of melting pot, the deposit account of the foreign exchange banker, it will thus be seen, reducing to a common denominator the various debts and claims on any foreign center existing at any one time.

The Question of Price

Why does the foreign exchange banker thus stand ready at any time either to buy or to sell? Because, naturally, there is a profit to be made on the operation. To reduce the matter to its very simplest and most understandable form, take the case of a foreign exchange banker in New York to whom there is offered, say, what he knows to be a perfectly good bill for £1000 drawn on some mercantile firm in London. He buys it, say, at a price of $3.50 per pound sterling, a total of $3500. A little later some one comes in and wants to buy a banker's draft on London for £1000. For this the banker charges him perhaps $3.52 per pound, a total of $3520, thus making a profit of $20 on the operation. Very likely the two drafts go forward to London on the same steamer, the commercial draft to be credited to the New York banker's London deposit account and the banker's draft sold by him to be debited thereto. In New York the foreign exchange banker took in $20 more than he paid out. In London, after the crediting and debiting of his sterling account is completed, every thing stands exactly as before.

Without attempting at this point fully to go into the matter, it may perhaps here be properly pointed out that different kinds of bills of exchange drawn on the same city command different prices in the exchange market. A bill drawn by a great bank in New York on a great bank in London is, obviously, bound to be salable at a higher price than a bill drawn by some merchant here on some merchant abroad, regardless of how good the credit of either or both parties to the transaction may be. From which fact, of course, arises the opportunity for profit on the part of the foreign exchange banker. Perfectly good and perfectly sure to be promptly paid on presentation as some bill drawn against a shipment of wheat or cotton or steel may be known to be, it is plain that the man who has it to sell is going to have to accept a slightly lower price for it than if it were a draft drawn by a bank on another bank. That type of paper, naturally, is bound always to command the best possible price.

The illustration used above of the sale of a banker's sight draft "against" a commercial sight draft was chosen merely as the simplest possible illustration of the part played by the foreign exchange banker in bringing together the man who has a draft to buy and the man who has a draft to sell. His operations, naturally, often assume a far more varied character. Always, however, the principle holds good that what the foreign exchange banker is trying to do is to put pounds or marks or francs into his deposit account in some foreign city at a less cost to himself in dollars than he can sell his own drafts for. Whatever the form or kind of the drafts offered to him, provided of course that he considers them to be *good*, they are all grist to his mill. The price he will pay for one kind of draft will naturally vary from the price he will pay for another; but, as long as he can see the chance of profitably selling his own draft against the balance to be created by the bills he is buying, he will not hesitate to buy.

Considerations That Govern

With regard to this question of the price the banker will pay for the bills offered to him, it may be observed in passing that there are at least two major considerations which govern. The first is the credit standing of the drawer of the bill and of the drawee. The second is the "usance" of the bill, the length of time which it has to run. A bill drawn "at sight," naturally (in which case the holder gets his money as soon as it is presented for payment), will command a better price than a bill according to the terms of which the drawee is given sixty days or even three or four months in which to pay. A "sight" or "demand" draft purchased by the banker and sent over to his correspondent is, almost immediately, credited to his account. The proceeds of a "time" draft, also, it is true, are credited to his account without delay, but only after such draft has been "discounted" in the open market. Which process of course, depending as the "discount rate" is high or low, will result in a larger or smaller number of pounds or francs or whatever it is being deducted from the face of the draft before it is credited to the remitting banker's account. Here, too, in the case of a "time draft" the question of credit becomes doubly important. Even though "discounted" at once and passed along to some third party, the endorsement of the banker who originally bought the bill from its maker remains on the bill for its entire life and keeps him liable until it has been actually presented and paid.

That being the case, it is plain that the "spread" in price, always considerable, between bills payable on demand and bills payable in two or three months, tends greatly to widen when there is the slightest question as to the stability of financial conditions at the center on which the bill is drawn. The "cable transfer," described a little further on, is naturally the form of exchange least affected by this consideration, the tie-up there being for only a few hours. Drafts pay-

able on demand, between the purchase and the en-
cashing of which a period of approximately one week
is likely to intervene, come next. "Long" bills, bills
payable anywhere from two to four months after
presentation, are naturally the most affected. So much
so, as a matter of fact, that if conditions at some given
center are known to be in an unsettled state, the drawing of "long" bills on that point becomes virtually impossible. No banker, palpably, is going to pay any
kind of price for a bill even on a bank, let alone on
a mercantile house, located in some city where serious
financial trouble is suspected to exist. Hardly for the
sake of the really very moderate profit to be made is
he going to allow his endorsement to go on a piece of
paper about whose "fate," as it is called, he has the
slightest doubt, and where the determination of that
"fate" must necessarily be postponed from two to
four months from the time the commitment is made.

Nor, on the other hand, is the foreign exchange
banker going to be willing to buy bills, either long or
short, unless he is aware of a demand for remittances
which makes him sure that he can sell his own bills
against the balance created by the bills he has bought.
Let a condition develop where it is all claims and no
debts (in other words where everyone has drafts to
sell and nobody needs drafts with which to make
remittances), and quickly enough the banks which
usually buy exchange will be found to have withdrawn
entirely from the market.

One other phase of the relationship of the foreign
exchange banker to the seller and the buyer of bills

remains to be mentioned: Theoretically the exchange banker is a *dealer* in bills, deriving his profit solely from what happens to be the prevailing differential between the price of the bills he buys and the bills he sells, and maintaining his balance abroad only at the amount necessary for the proper clearance of the transactions. Practically, he is sometimes that and sometimes himself a speculator on the rate of exchange. He may feel, for instance, that rates are rising. In that case he is likely to sell his own drafts against only a part of what he is buying, his balance abroad being thus allowed to accumulate. Or, on the other hand, if he figures the market as having a downward trend, he is likely to sell more heavily than he buys, his balance abroad being thus allowed to run down. So far, indeed, may this latter process be carried that he will even overdraw his balance abroad, figuring that before the time the drafts he has sold arrive on the other side and are presented for payment, he will have replenished his balance through the transfer of funds by cable.

Transfer by Cable

Cable transfers are, of course, in every essential the same as any other form of order for the payment of money. In the case of a draft the instructions to pay are written out on an oblong piece of paper and signed; in the case of a cable transfer they are sent by wire in a prearranged and carefully guarded code —that is the only difference. Except, of course, that where a banker sells a cable transfer the funds are immediately paid out by the correspondent bank abroad according to instructions; whereas, in the case of a draft on London, for instance, the English bank makes no payment to anybody until the draft is presented at its window a week or more after it was written and signed. If, thus, there can be said to be any difference at all, it is simply that in the case of a cable transfer the instructions to pay are received by the paying bank sooner than in the case of a draft, written out and signed and sent by mail.

Naturally, therefore, on account of this element of time, the cable transfer commands a slightly better price (rate of exchange) than does the sight draft. The man buying a cable transfer pays out his money on one end and, almost immediately, the money is paid out on the other end to the party designated by him; there being thus not only no loss of interest, but the time during which anything unfavorable might happen to the paying bank abroad being reduced to an absolute minimum. The man buying a sight draft, on the other hand, pays out his money and for fully a week has nothing to show for it but a piece of paper.

Nature of the "Long Bill"

Several times in the foregoing pages reference has been made to bills described as "long," bills payable in sixty or more days from the time of their being presented to the drawee for his "acceptance." The nature of a "draft payable on demand" of course requires no explanation and in the preceding paragraphs, the "cable transfer" was fully described. There remains then only to be touched on the nature of "long bill," one of the most important instruments in foreign exchange, by the way, and one of the least generally understood.

We shall perhaps most easily arrive at a true understanding of the nature of the long bill of exchange if we bear consistently in mind the fact that in foreign as in domestic commerce comparatively little merchandise is sold on a spot cash basis. Almost always, where sales are of any size and between parties enjoying first class credit, the arrangement is that the buyer is to have a period of time running anywhere from two to four months in which to make payment. Such arrangement, in the case of domestic commerce, is likely to take the form of an open "book account" or of a "trade acceptance." Where the shipment is to be made overseas, it is likely to take the form of an agreement between seller and buyer that the seller's draft on the buyer is not to be made payable "at sight" or "on demand," but that it is to be made payable sixty days, ninety days or even four months after presentation to and "acceptance" by the party on whom it is drawn.

Assuming then that the merchandise will arrive not much after the draft is presented for acceptance, it is plain that the buyer of the goods will have a period of anything up to four months in which to make payment. Yet, as we have seen, the shipper, the maker of the draft, sells it just as soon as he has made it and thus receives payment for his goods. The buyer of the goods hasn't paid for them and won't pay for them for several months and yet the seller has received payment. Someone else, it is plain, has stepped in and for the time being, at least, put up the money. Who?

The foreign exchange banker in New York, of course, who originally bought the draft from the maker; and, after him, the party in London to whom the draft, after having been "accepted" by the drawee, was sold. *Where* did the money come from? From the "discount market," evidently, from that great reservoir of fluid bank capital which in a center like London is always seeking the chance of investment in just such forms of "paper." Following its acceptance the bill was at once "discounted"—sold to somebody at something off its face value—by the London agent of the American foreign exchange banker. In the hands of that first buyer it may have remained until due; or, on the other hand, during the term of its life, it may have been sold to a second buyer and by him possibly to a third, each time of course less the current rate of interest for the remaining unexpired period. Discounted and rediscounted perhaps several times in the great "open market"; presented finally by the last holder for payment when due; a loan, virtually, by the discount market to the buyer of the merchandise; that, essentially, is the nature, the life story of the long bill.

In the first chapter there was discussed the circumstances originating inter-country debts and claims; in the second, the practical method of their settlement. With these facts, then, as to foreign currency drafts and how they originate clearly in mind, we are in a position finally to go ahead with our consideration of that all-important question, the "rate-of-exchange" —that is to say the price of the money of one country expressed in terms of the money of another country. What makes the pound, the franc, the dollar and the other currencies fall and rise in terms of one another —that is the next thing which we shall have to consider.

CHAPTER III

THE RATE OF EXCHANGE

A BILL of exchange, we have just seen, is really nothing more nor less than a form of instruction to a bank or business house in some foreign country to pay to the party named in the bill a specified amount of foreign currency at a specified time. As in the case of any other form of property, therefore, (bonds, for example, which also are an order to receive money) bills of exchange are the subject, at constantly varying prices, of purchase and sale. When bills are being freely offered the price goes down; when bills are wanted the price goes up. All of which, of course, is only another way of saying that the ruling price of any kind of a bill of exchange at any given time is simply the result of the law of supply and demand.

What then is known as the "rate of exchange" between two countries is the *price* of bills drawn in the currency of one expressed in terms of the currency of the other. The statement, for example, that the rate of exchange on Paris is 3.94 means simply that the *price* of a banker's draft drawn on Paris in francs would be 3.94 American cents for each franc.

Given a time when the demand for drafts on some foreign point was exactly equal to the supply, we should, of course, have no fluctuation whatever in the rate of exchange. That, however, at least in the case of any two primary markets, never happens. Where so many debts and so many claims are in constant course of being settled, it is invariably the case that a greater amount of "exchange" is wanted than is available; or, on the other hand, that the supply of bills exceeds the demand. The inevitable result of which of course is that, as the case may be, the price which the would-be buyers have to pay is increased or the price which the would-be sellers have to accept is lessened.

Just here, at the very beginning of our inquiry into the question of what makes rates go up and down, we want to be very sure that we understand that both demand and supply in the case of bills of exchange, as in the case of anything else, are to a certain extent a consequence of immediately current prices. At the rate we mentioned of 3.94 for bills on Paris the supply at any given time may amount to so-and-so-many francs and the demand may be for so-and-so-many. Let the rate increase, say to 3.94⅛, and a change in the picture begins to take place. Immediately a certain proportion of those who were buyers at 3.94 drop out; while, on the other hand, others who were not willing to sell at the lower figure come in and make offerings. Seemingly almost too simple and elementary to consider, and only of course what happens wherever any form of property is bought and sold at a price, this increase in the supply as rates go up and this increase in the demand as they go down is, nevertheless, something a full appreciation of which will be found a very great help in understanding the movement of the exchanges. Many a transaction in exchange has gone wrong because of lack of appreciation that conditions of demand and supply with exchange at one price may be entirely different from those conditions with the rate of exchange at a level even only slightly different.

Nature of a "Rate of Exchange"

Another and even more important thing to be kept constantly in mind when considering this question of the movement of exchange rates is that there are two ends to every rate of exchange—two places where the price of that particular exchange is determined. If one end of a seesaw starts to go up it is not necessarily by any means because weight has been removed from that end. Weight added to the other end would, of course, produce exactly the same effect. If, then, there is a sudden rise in New York say in the exchange rate on London, it will not be sufficient for us to seek the cause of that rise in New York alone. Very possibly the rise in the rate is due not at all to anything that has happened in New York but is the result solely of something that has happened in London.

Again, the illustration of the seesaw may be made to stand us in good stead in the pursuit of our inquiry into what may be called the "two-endedness" of exchange rates. Just as when one end of a seesaw goes down the other goes up, so when on one end an exchange rate goes up, on the other end it goes down. At some given time, we will say, the rate of exchange on London, in New York is $3.50, that is to say, banker's drafts on London are quoted at $3.50 per

pound sterling. The rate in New York, we will now
assume, rises to $3.60. What happens in London?
The rate there, too, of course, goes to $3.60, but
whereas what happened in New York was a *rise* in the
rate on London, what happened in London was a
fall in the rate on New York. In New York, after
what took place, pounds sterling cost more than they
did before, ten cents more. In London, on the other
hand, whereas previously a pound sterling bought only
$3.50 in the form of a draft on New York, now that
same pound sterling buys $3.60.

If any misapprehension of the above by any chance
remains, it will, perhaps, best be cleared up by consideration of the fact that between two markets in
close cable communication it is obviously impossible
that there should at any time be any material difference in the quotation for exchange. With the pound
quoted in New York at $3.50, for example, the pound
in London will necessarily be quoted at or exceedingly
close to the same figure—that is to say, the pound
in London will buy $3.50, no less no more, in the way
of a draft on New York. Suppose, for purposes of
illustration, that it were *not* so; that, at a time when
drafts on London could be bought in New York at
$3.50 per pound sterling, the pound in London would
buy say as much as $3.51 or $3.52 in the way of a
draft on New York. Must it not be clear that instantly there would be a rush in New York to buy
sterling drafts on London (cost, $3.50 per pound),
which drafts, when sent over to London, could be
used to buy dollar drafts on New York at the rate of
$3.51 or $3.52 per pound? To be able to buy some-

thing for $3.50 which could immediately be re-converted into $3.51 or $3.52 would indeed be a "sweet" operation and one of which exchange dealers in both cities would hardly be slow to take advantage. Assuming that the condition outlined could ever develop at all, any such discrepancy in rates would be very quickly ironed out by the buying of sterling in New York and the selling of sterling in London which would immediately take place. Immediately, of course, as it would be through the buying and selling of cable transfers rather than of demand drafts that the operations would be conducted.

Ready at last, perhaps, to proceed with our examination of the conditions which cause exchange rates to go up and down, we shall do well no doubt to fix on some one definite point and to confine our consideration to the conditions there actually prevailing. The same principles, it is true, activate the rise and fall of the exchange at any given financial center. Choosing some one point, however, and sticking to that, we shall possibly avoid at least some of the difficulties inherent in a discussion conducted entirely in generalities. Let us take then, say, New York, and for the purposes of the current discussion, confine our examination to conditions at that point as they affect the rise and fall of the exchange on the world's other great financial centers.

Merchandise Exports

Beginning with the conditions which tend to depress exchange rates, first place unquestionably must be given to those occasional but frequently recurring periods of heavy merchandise exports which are wont to flood the market with offerings of bills of exchange often at the very time when the demand for remittance is at a minimum. Each year at the end of the summer, for example, when cotton shipments begin to go forward in quantity, we see this condition develop. Pre-sale to bankers of a certain proportion of these "cotton drafts" may, it is true, have been made in the form of "futures" for weeks and perhaps even months before the bills are actually drawn; but, even so, the amount of bills which come in and are sold at whatever is the best price currently obtainable is likely to prove a serious depressant on rates. Particularly so as within a comparatively short time after the movement of cotton bills into the exchange market gets under full headway, bills drawn against grain and all sorts of other agricultural produce begin to come in for sale.

Without departing from our idea of confining ourselves to the New York market in our examination of what makes exchange rates rise and fall, we may well note in passing how much more of an influence on exchange rates a sudden flood of merchandise exports is certain to exert at some lesser center (where perhaps there may at the moment be little or no demand for remittance) than at an important point like New York, where at all times more or less of such a demand does exist. Take, for instance, a small "one crop" country like Guatemala, where the coffee crop matures and is exported all within a comparatively short space of time, with the result that the market is flooded with offerings of sterling and dollar drafts. Unless, at the time, it happens, which is very unlikely, that imports into Guatemala are running on a very heavy scale, the disposal of the coffee drafts is likely to prove very much of a problem. The exchange rate, of course, is bound to be most adversely affected.

Security Exports

Next in importance to these periods of large merchandise exports as an influence on exchange rates come the times when Europe is buying securities heavily in the New York market. In the sharpness of its incidence on exchange rates, indeed, this influence at times transcends all others. In buying movements of this sort that last any length of time, it must be remembered, the amounts involved are enormous. The purchase of a single thousand shares of stock selling even as low as in the thirties involves the drawing and sale of a draft for approximately £10,000; the purchase of a block of a hundred bonds, of approximately £30,000. These foreign buying movements of our securities, moreover, are apt to be of a concentrated character. The statement that "Europe is buying" is not so apt to mean that foreign investors in general have become favorably inclined toward our securities and disposed gradually to pick them up when offered at material concessions. It can mean that and at times does; but, more usually, it means that large financial interests abroad have made up their minds that security prices here are about to rise and that they are coming in to do their buying in anticipation. Such purchases, of course, are carefully and discriminatingly made, but, unless the market "runs away" in such a fashion as completely to check the enthusiasm of the prospective buyers, are likely to run into large volume. Even with conditions upset as they have been during the past few years, the buying power latent in European financial centers is very large indeed, and of what might be called a concentrated character by reason of the fact that so much investing abroad is done through the medium of the investment trust. Purchases here, therefore, particularly when countries like England, Holland and Switzerland really start buying our securities, are not apt to be made in driblets but are much more apt to take the form of orders for sizable amounts. And, when to this foreign investment trust buying there is added the speculative buying by foreign banking interests by which it is nearly always accompanied, there is likely to be an aggregate of purchases of tremendous size.

Payment for securities so purchased is almost invariably made by having the seller here or his bank draw on the buyer abroad (or on the buyer's bank.) Small wonder then that when one of these inter-country security buying movements gets under way, the market where the buying is taking place is apt to be flooded with offerings of demand bills. Purchases of securities, it must be remembered, are not, like purchase of merchandise, made on any sort of a credit basis. The New York stock or bond broker receiving an order from London or Amsterdam to buy a quarter of a million dollars' worth of Atchison Fours or five thousand shares of Steel wants his money and wants it at once. "Buy and draw on us," reads the cable and that is what he does—pounds sterling on London, Swiss francs on Zurich, guilders on Amsterdam, as the case may be. Does the market for the particular kind of bill he is drawing happen to be depressed, he simply increases the face amount of his draft. Reimbursement for his outlay is, after all, what he is interested in rather than any rate of exchange; the right to draw (or to have his bank draw) a bill of exchange which, when sold, will yield him as many dollars, plus commission, as he paid for the securities he is shipping to his client.

Flotation abroad of American bond issues have, of course, an effect on exchange rates similar to that exerted by these periodic buying excursions into the American securities market. Formerly of great importance in the days when America had to rely largely on foreign capital, this influence is to-day making itself less and less felt. Sale of entire American bond issues of any size abroad is probably a thing of the past, though, of course, it is a fact that European banks still participate with American banks in the bringing out of new issues. Following one of these flotations in which the foreign banks are taking a sizable interest, there is apt to be some increase in offerings of exchange; but in its effect on rates this influence is one which to-day seldom attains any great degree of importance. Even in the case of a 25 or 50 million dollar issue the total amount taken for foreign account is apt to be too small to exert any very great effect on rates. Particularly as in transactions of this kind between large banks, which are a very different sort of thing from orders given to American brokers to buy and ship stocks, the drawing of the reimbursing drafts is likely to be deferred until conditions favorable to their disposal obtain.

Inter-Market Short Term Loans

The third influence tending to depress rates is, like the influence described in the preceding paragraph, one which in former years counted for a good deal more than it does now but which must nevertheless be set down in its place in a work designed to cover basically the principles on which the exchange markets work. Reference is made to the sudden and substantial supplies of bills of exchange which come into the market whenever foreign short term loans are being made here on any considerable scale. With the rate for money 5% here, we will say, as against 3% in London, a strong incentive comes into existence for the foreign banks to use their money on this side rather than on the other, and arrangements begin to be made to extend short term loans of English money to the American market. How is this done? By the old familiar method of having the borrowing bank in New York draw its drafts in sterling on the lending bank in London. These drafts will then be sold in the American exchange market for dollars, the seller being thus provided with the equivalent, in usable form, of the pounds sterling which he has borrowed.

But do not the drafts so drawn, it may well be asked, have to be paid, thus re-absorbing the loanable dollars which were provided by their sale? Such, of course, *would* be the case were the drafts made payable "at sight" or "on demand"; but, as it happens, in the making of these short term foreign loans the drafts are never drawn at sight but always for sixty days or ninety days or whatever is the time which has been agreed upon as the life of the loan. The New York borrower who has made and sold the draft is thus under no necessity of at once turning back the funds he has realized, but is in a position to enjoy their use until the drafts come due and he has to make provision for paying them off.

This whole question of the drawing of drafts which accompanies the loaning of short term foreign money in this market is here brought in only because of its influence on exchange rates and not with the idea of entering upon any full description at this point of the details of the operation. One point, however, must be definitely understood if we are to have a clear idea of the effect of such operations on exchange rates and that is that whereas the bills of exchange which come into existence when the loans are made are drawn at sixty or ninety days sight and must be sold for dollars *at the lower rate of exchange prevailing for "long" drafts,* the eventual actual payment of the drafts must be made with sight drafts or cables, obtainable, of course, *only at a considerably higher price.* The difference, naturally, is the cost of the accommodation to the borrower.

At a time when foreign money is being loaned in this market on an extensive scale, then, large amounts of sixty and ninety-day drafts come into existence and are thrown on the exchange market for sale. Is the effect, it may be asked, the same as if the drafts were drawn at sight or demand? Practically the same, the answer is, for the simple reason that sixty and ninety day bills can be used for purposes of remittance just about as well as demand drafts or cables. "Long" bills used for that purpose will, of course, have to be discounted when they arrive in London; but all that that means from a practical standpoint is that for the discharging of a given debt a slightly larger number of pounds will have to be sent over than would be the case if demand exchange were used. So-and-so-many pounds purchased at a certain rate—a slightly larger number of pounds purchased at a rate slightly lower—the proposition is as broad as it is long.

Passing on from consideration of the effect on exchange rates of short term loans made *to* us to consideration of short term loans made *by* us, it is evident that it is not when these latter are made but when they come due and are paid off by the borrowers abroad that a depressing effect is exerted on the exchange market here. London has been borrowing heavily here, we will say, through the drawing and sale of sixty and ninety day bills drawn in dollars on American banks and the time for repayment has come. What happens then? One of two things: Either we begin a large scale drawing of sight drafts in sterling on the borrowers abroad or, what amounts to the same thing, they are under the necessity of going into their own exchange market and securing large amounts of drafts drawn in dollars for remittance to this side. That, of course, tends to force up the price of dollar drafts in London, which, as we have seen, is only another way of saying to force down the price of sterling drafts in New York. Why, oh, why, asks the cotton shipper in New Orleans or the meat shipper in Chicago, am I getting such a miserably low rate for the perfectly good bills I am drawing against my shipments and sending to New York for sale? Very possibly, Mr. Shipper, because it just happens to be a time when a lot of bankers here in New York are drawing and offering their own sterling bills and when a lot of other bankers over in London are under the necessity of buying dollar drafts on a large scale in order to pay off loans they have maturing in New York.

Deposit Withdrawals

Finally, in our examination of the various influences tending to depress exchange rates, we come down to what is perhaps the simplest and most evident of them all, the withdrawal on a large scale by the bankers of one country of the funds they have on deposit in another. Always and at all times, as we have seen, as a condition incident to the conduct of an international banking business, the banks here carry large deposit accounts (sterling balances) with their correspondents in London and the banks in London do the same thing (dollar balances) with the banks here. Varying in size, of course, seasonally and otherwise, these deposit accounts, even at the lowest point to which they are ever drawn down, run in the aggregate into very big figures. It just has to be so. Without being prepared at a moment's notice either to draw or to be drawn on for substantial amounts, no bank claiming to be seriously engaged in inter-country financing would be in a position to offer any worth-while kind of service to its clients.

Now with exchange rates fluctuating as they do, it is perfectly evident that there will be times when the New York banks, for example, will be disposed to let the balances they are carrying in London and Paris and Amsterdam and other foreign points build up to large proportions; and that there will be other times when they will be disposed to draw them down to the greatest possible extent. Such balances, remember, are in foreign currency, and as the price of that currency (the exchange rate) rises or falls, become more valuable or less valuable, as the case may be, when reckoned in dollars. Obviously, then, if a bank figures that the exchange rate on some given point is going to rise, it will increase the balances it is carrying at that point; while, if the prospect is for a fall in rates, it will diminish its foreign balances to the lowest point consonant with the arrangement it has with its foreign depository regarding the maintenance of balances, etc.

The threat of serious financial disturbances at any given point, naturally, is likely to result in the recall, on an extensive scale, of balances carried at that point by banks and bankers in other countries. Nor is it necessary, for this to take place, that there exist any real serious doubt as to the solvency of the banks at the point of deposit. Let there develop, for instance, the slightest possibility that there may be put into effect at the point where the funds are on deposit anything in the way of restrictive measures on the free movement of gold, and, almost instantly, extensive withdrawals of balances will begin to take place. Nobody, not even that altruistic soul known as the international banker, wants to keep his funds on deposit at a point from which he is not sure he can withdraw them when, as and if he sees fit.

A time then when for any reason or combination of reasons deposits at some foreign point are being withdrawn on an extensive scale is bound to be a time when drafts on that point are being freely offered and sold. Such drawing and selling of drafts, however, it is particularly to be noted, will not necessarily take place at the point where the funds are owned and to which they are being withdrawn. Take a case, for instance, where New York bankers, desirous for any given reason of withdrawing down their balances in London, find that the demand for sterling drafts drawn on London is very much better in Paris than it is in New York. What, in that case, would be the procedure? Obviously not to draw sterling drafts in New York and sell them at a poor price in a falling market, but rather to direct that the drawing on London be done from Paris, at which point a good market for such drafts was known to exist. What happens then is this: Paris, as directed from New York, draws on London, New York's sterling deposits in London being thus converted into franc deposits in Paris. Gradually, then, as the market for franc drafts in New York allows, these funds are recalled from Paris through the drawing and sale of drafts on that point. With regard to the advantage of doing it that way, remember, it is one thing to draw and try to sell drafts in a market where everyone else is trying to do the same thing in a hurry, and something quite different to draw and dispose of exchange on a point at which no disturbance exists.

The Reverse Side

Turning now from consideration of the things which at a point like New York make exchange rates go down, to consideration of the things which make them go up, it might perhaps at first be thought that the one set of circumstances is bound to be simply the converse of the other. Such, however, as a little careful examination of the facts of the matter will show, is very often far from being the case.

Beginning with the question of the interchange of merchandise, we saw how, because our exports are to so large an extent agricultural (and thus seasonal) exchange rates are much more affected at certain times of the year than at others. A similar condition, in the case of *imports,* does not prevail, there being no particular period when imports run materially heavier than at any other period. Special circumstances such, for instance, as the imminence of the imposition of increased tariff schedules may at times result in a certain stimulation of imports, but hardly to an extent sufficient materially to affect the rate of exchange. Generally speaking, imports into the United States are of so varied a character that they are pretty evenly distributed over the year and there is no one season when they can be counted upon to run more heavily than at any other.

We are, of course, speaking of New York and the

American market. In the case of many lesser markets the situation is entirely different. Reference has been previously made to countries like Guatemala whose exports are mostly made at one time of the year and whose imports likewise are of a highly seasonal character. Such a condition, naturally, results in alternating periods of scarcity and plethora of bills of exchange. During the time that the coffee crop is going out the market there may be flooded with offerings of sterling and dollar drafts while, only a few months later, the arrival of several successive heavy shipments of merchandise may result in the creation of such a heavy demand for sterling and dollar drafts that importers there are hard put to it to find the means of making remittances in payment of what they have bought. The local banks in that case have to step in and for the time being themselves carry the load by selling to the importers who so much need them their own sixty and ninety drafts on New York. This the banks are able to do by reason of the fact that the Federal Reserve Board recognizes the need for bank financing of this sort at certain foreign points to take care of imports from the United States, and has indeed published a list of the countries which it considers entitled to acceptance facilities of this sort. Needless to say, the drawing of such time drafts for the purpose of supplying legitimately needed exchange and thus preventing too violent fluctuations in rates is confined to banks and bankers. The maximum "usance" of such bills, furthermore, is three months nor are they subject to renewal. The idea of course is that before the three months elapse and the drafts have actually to be paid, exports of coffee or other commodities will have provided a supply of exchange out of which payment of these bank drafts can be effected.

Import of Securities

Merchandise imports, we have seen, being steady as they are, are not likely at an important point like New York to cause violent fluctuations in exchange. Security imports are an entirely different proposition. Europe since the Great War has of course borrowed rather than lent money here, but prior to that time for a period of almost three quarters of a century European capital flowed into American industry in a steady stream with the result that at the time the War broke out Europe's holdings of American stocks and bonds ran into the billions. No record of the amount is available nor is there any way of telling by how much on balance these foreign holdings have since been reduced. Very certain, however, it is that even making the fullest allowance for what we have bought back during the past ten or fifteen years, the sum total of American stocks and bonds owned abroad still runs to an enormous figure.

Definite appreciation of this fact is necessary to a clear understanding of how the foreign exchange market in New York is periodically affected when for any reason whatever a selling movement in "Americans," or "Yankees" as they are sometimes called, sets in. Europe, as we have seen, still has times when she *buys* "Americans," with the result that sterling is sharply depressed; but even the most extensive of such buying movements are as nothing to what happens to the other side of the international ledger when Europe really starts in to sell. So great are the British, Dutch, French, Swiss and other holdings of American stocks and bonds that a selling wave calculated to reduce these holdings by even only a small percentage means the dumping into this market of an aggregate running into the scores of millions. Which, of course, means that at such times the problem of finding sufficient exchange with which to make payment for all these securities so repurchased becomes a serious one indeed.

With regard to the effect on inter-country security purchases and sales of a greatly depressed rate of exchange, that subject must properly be left to a later chapter. At this point, however, it may well be noted that when a main rate of exchange, as for instance sterling, stands at a low figure, the effect is to greatly stimulate sales of British-held American securities. The pound sterling, after all, remains the pound sterling in London, whatever the exchange rate with any foreign country may be. When therefore the Englishman holding an American dollar stock or bond can possess himself of a pound sterling by selling say only $4 worth of his securities where normally in order to get that pound it was necessary for him to sell nearly $5 worth, the incentive to do so is very great indeed. And the lower the rate of exchange, naturally, the greater the incentive becomes.

Lending Abroad

When short term loans are being made *to* us, we saw, sterling and other drafts are drawn by us on the lending banks abroad and the available supply of exchange is largely increased. When short term loans are being made *by* us, the situation of course is exactly reversed. A time when we are lending largely on the other side, in other words, is a time when sixty and ninety day dollar drafts on New York are being freely drawn and offered for sale in European centers. That, naturally, works toward weakness in the rate for dollars there and toward strength in the rate for pounds and francs here.

Continuous effort has been made in the preparation of this book to keep it a discussion of basic principles and not of conditions currently prevailing in exchange. Without, however, departing from that principle in any way, it may be pointed out that with regard to this business of inter-country short term loans the situation has completely changed in recent years and that whereas in former times Europe's loaning of short term money in this market was on a grand scale, it is we who to-day are doing most of the loaning. Before and up to the time of the War it was the well-stocked capital markets of London, Paris and Amsterdam which always had a surplus to lend and upon whose lending institutions American banks and bankers were always drawing their sixty and ninety day bills. Now, however, the situation is entirely different. Europe at present (and this situation seems likely so to remain for years to come) needs every dollar of her available capital, and instead of being as formerly a lender is to-day steadily on the borrowing side. So far, then, as the exchange market is concerned, it is not the bankers' long sterling and franc draft which is the major influence, but, rather, the bankers' long dollar draft drawn from abroad on New York.

Such being the case, it follows that whereas the maturing of short term loans made by us often results in a demand for dollar drafts at foreign points sufficient sharply to affect the rate of exchange (to put it up there and consequently down here), no such influence is exerted by the coming due of the comparatively small loans made by European bankers in the American market. Formerly, as has been said, all that was very different; and the development of money market conditions abroad leading to unwillingness on the part of foreign lenders to consent to "renewal" was often the signal for a sharp run-up in sterling and other rates. Now, however, that never happens for the simple reason that the total of bankers' sterling and other long drafts outstanding at any one time in New York has become so small that repayment, whenever that becomes necessary, can be effected without the causing of anything more than a ripple in rates.

"Re-patriation" of Funds

Finally, coming down to the question of the effect of the withdrawal of funds carried on deposit here, it will at once be evident that if there has been a great diminution in the amount of banking capital Europe has available for loaning in the American market, so the amounts which the foreign banks are able to keep on deposit here must also be measurably less. Such, indeed, is the case. For the normal conduct of the business they do with us the foreign banks have, of course, to carry deposits here of sizable amount; but, except when conditions in the home market are temporarily unfavorable for the loaning of money, such deposits are likely to be held down pretty well to a "necessity" basis.

That being so, it will readily appear that even a time when the foreign banks are disposed to bring home any surplus they may have on deposit in New York, is by no means necessarily a time of scarcity of bills and high rates of exchange. Standing arrangements to keep on deposit with a correspondent a stipulated minimum amount are not to be lightly disturbed. In the aggregate, of course, the amount of foreign deposits here is considerable, and the development of conditions making for urgent recall has at times been sufficient to cause more or less of a flurry in exchange rates. Duration of such a condition is not, however, apt to be long. Fears are proved to be unfounded or the urgent need at home for funds subsides; after which the deposits are returned and things go on as before.

The above, of course, refers to the deposit relationship of privately owned banks. When we come to the inter-operation of the Government Banks, the case is entirely different. Whereas, indeed, the amount kept on deposit in New York by foreign private banks and bankers is measurably less, the amount so kept on deposit by the various Central Banks of Europe is very much greater than at any previous period. The Bank of France, for instance, as this is written, has on deposit in the City of New York a sum in excess of half a billion dollars. No one other foreign government has on deposit here an amount even approaching such a figure; but in the aggregate the deposits here of the various European Central Banks run up nowadays to a very considerable sum.

As long as these deposits are allowed to remain where they are or in any case are drawn upon only moderately, no great influence is exerted on exchange rates one way or the other. When, however, as during the early months of 1932, a movement sets in to bring these balances home, the effect on the exchange market can become very pronounced indeed. Particularly so if, as was the case at that time, the recalling of these very large balances comes at a time when newly erected tariff barriers by France and these other nations has happened to reduce our merchandise exports to them to a point where the supply of franc and other exchange is no more than is necessary to meet the current demand. To inject into such a situation an insistent buying of bills by these foreign banks anxious to re-patriate their American deposits is to all intents and purposes to make it certain that rates will be driven up to the highest point to which it is possible for them to rise. In the very presence then of these foreign Central Bank deposits—and, of course, more particularly, in the possibility of their withdrawal—we have what cannot be regarded as other than one of the most potent of exchange market influences.

Attempt was made in the first paragraphs of the foregoing chapter to show how the rate of exchange between two countries is really nothing more nor less than the price of the currency of one country expressed in terms of the currency of the other. Following that, it was shown how any rate of exchange is necessarily affected by conditions prevailing not only in one but in both countries concerned. New York was then chosen for purposes of illustration of these principles and there were set forth (1) the circumstances which at that financial center cause exchange rates to fall and (2) the circumstances which cause them to rise. Following which general discussion of "exchange" and what makes it go up and down, we are ready, perhaps, to proceed with a somewhat closer examination of rates and their actual fluctuation. With this necessarily more or less academic viewpoint established, very possibly we shall be able to get a clearer view of just how rates actually do move, of how far they move, and of what happens when they reach the absolute limit of their possible fluctuation either on the down or the up side.

CHAPTER IV

GOLD, THE INTERNATIONAL CURRENCY

IN any country doing business on a substantial scale with other countries there are at all times, we have seen, people who owe money abroad and thus are under the necessity of buying foreign exchange with which to make their payments; and other people to whom money is owed from abroad and who are thus in a position to offer for sale the bills of exchange which they are all the time drawing on the people who owe them money. Allowing for the fact that supply and demand will never be exactly in balance and that there will thus always be a certain amount of variation in the price at which the purchaser of bills must buy and the price at which the seller of bills must sell, it is nevertheless a fact, as we have seen, that under normal conditions there are always bills which can be bought at a price and that there is always a price at which bills can be sold. Under *normal* conditions, be it noted. What we have now to consider is what happens when the balance swings so far one way or the other that (1) there are no bills to be had at any price (2) that offerings of bills find no buyers. How under those circumstances does the man who owes money abroad make payment? How under those circumstances does the man who is owed from abroad get paid?

The answer, of course, is through the medium of gold, the international currency. At any time in any country gold can be readily exchanged for the currency of that country.

Gold and the Bill of Exchange

Essentially, between gold-using countries (to which this part of the discussion is necessarily confined) there is no difference whatever between a payment made by means of a bill of exchange and a payment made by means of a shipment of gold. What, after all, is a foreign draft on a bank in a gold standard country but an order addressed to that bank to pay out a certain amount of gold? Where settlement of an inter-country debt is made by means of a gold shipment, the specie is sent direct. Where settlement is made by means of a bill of exchange, the creditor abroad receives, instead of the physical specie, an order upon some local bank to deliver him specie. In the one case, payment is made direct. In the other it is made through the medium of a foreign bank. Essentially, it amounts to the same thing.

Payment by draft being so much easier and more convenient to all parties, however, that method, whenever possible, is invariably employed. Shipping gold back and forth across the ocean is a cumbersome and expensive operation. Perfectly feasible as a last resort way of settling an inter-country debt it will, nevertheless, be avoided as long as it is possible to settle the debt in any other way without too great additional expense. Let the price of the necessary bill of exchange, however, become excessive, and the alternative ceases to exist. If the payment has got to be made and no bill of exchange with which to make it is available, there remains nothing that the debtor can do except to ship the physical gold, or at least get his bank to do it for him.

Gold and the Foreign Exchange Bankers

At this point it is of the greatest importance to note that just as the payment of a debt in a foreign country is accomplished through the intervention of a foreign exchange banker, so, when settlement is made in the form of gold, the foreign exchange banker again comes into the picture. An American buyer of French silks, for instance, finding it necessary to make payment in the form of specie, would not himself undertake to ship gold to Paris. What he would do would be to go to some bank in New York and bid a price for the necessary franc draft which would induce the bank itself to ship the gold to its Paris correspondent, thus establishing for itself a deposit on which its own bill can be drawn. Actual shipment of gold, in other words, is not made directly by the debtor to the creditor, neither of whom, in any probability, have the necessary equipment for handling such transactions. What happens is that an intermediary bank is used for the purpose, and allowed a profit for the use of its facilities.

In actual practice, of course, the banks who make a specialty of bullion shipments do not accommodate individual buyers of exchange by shipping gold for them. What actually takes place is that as a concentrated demand for drafts on some foreign point forces the price of those drafts higher and higher, foreign exchange bankers begin to make preparations for shipping gold to that point for the purpose of establishing balances there on which they themselves can draw their drafts. At what point, then, does gold begin actually to go out? At the point, plainly, where the bankers can see a satisfactory profit in shipping gold and selling their drafts against the deposits so established. To establish a balance of so-and-so-many francs in Paris, the banker figures, will cost him so-an-so-many dollars. When therefore the price he is bid for drafts rises to such a point that he knows he will be able to sell out his newly created Paris balance for as much as it cost him to get it over there plus a satisfactory profit, the banker will begin to ship gold. And as long as he can continue to sell drafts at a price that show him a profit he will continue shipping gold. Why not? No capital is being tied up. With one hand he is buying gold. With the other he is selling his drafts and getting the money with which to pay for it.

Such being the case, it is evident that between two gold standard countries there is a very definite point beyond which the rate of exchange cannot rise for the very simple reason that at that point an unlimited supply of bills of exchange comes automatically into existence. Be the demand for bills of exchange what it may, as long as gold is available for shipment, as much exchange as is wanted is bound to be offered at a price no higher than the banker's cost of shipping the gold plus the banker's really very moderate profit. Surprisingly narrow, moreover, will be found to be the profit on which the banker is willing to work. Let the opportunity present itself here in New York for the banker to net $1,000 per $1,000,000 of gold shipped, and gold will freely flow out. So keen, indeed, is the competition among the big banks making a specialty of shipping gold, that even considerably before the exchange rate rises to a point which shows the above profit of one-tenth of one percent, gold exporting operations begin to get under way.

Convertibility into Gold

In a previous paragraph gold was referred to as the "international currency," as something which can at any time be converted into the currency of any country. It will now be well, perhaps, to look a little more specifically into the question of this ready convertibility of gold.

The unit of currency of all gold using countries contains a definitely prescribed amount of gold. Thus in the United States the pure gold content of the dollar is fixed by law at 23.22 grains. In France (law of June 25, 1928) the pure gold content of the franc is 58.95 milligrams. Each gold using country thus fixes by law the amount of pure gold which its unit of currency is to contain. To own, then, the amount of gold that is contained in a franc, for instance, or a dollar, is literally to own a franc or a dollar. In the United States, to take our own case, anyone owning 23.22 grains of pure gold (gold "1000 fine") can take it around to any Government Assay Office and get a dollar for it. If he wishes, the Government will coin each 232.20 grains he has into a ten-dollar gold piece. Or, if he prefers, the Government will simply buy his gold from him at the fixed price of one dollar for 23.22 grains ($20.67 per troy ounce). Gold so purchased by the Government may be coined, or on the other hand may be made up into the form of bars for sale to exporters or to users of the metal in the arts.

What, it may at this point well be asked, is the status of this matter in a country like England which, at the time this is written, temporarily has suspended its law fixing the gold value of the pound sterling? Simply that the number of pounds sterling that a given amount of gold will buy is the same number of pounds sterling that could be bought with the franc- or dollar- (or other currency) equivalent of the amount of gold in question. No longer does the English owner of gold exchange it for pounds sterling at the old price of 7.3224 grams of fine gold per pound. What he exchanges it for is the amount of pounds sterling that could be bought with the number of, say, dollars or francs that could be secured with each 7.3224 grams of pure gold he happens to have. As a matter of fact, almost needless to say, no exchange into dollars or francs, followed by conversion into pounds, actually takes place. What really happens is that, as American and French exchange on London rises and falls, so the "premium" on gold in London falls and rises, and the conversion of the gold is made into sterling at this premium, whatever at the moment it happens to be.

The Par of Exchange

While on this question of the gold value of various currencies it will be well, perhaps, to note the meaning of that much misunderstood and misused term, the "mint par of exchange" between two countries. For purposes of illustration, let us take the United States and France. The U. S. dollar, we have seen, contains 23.22 grains of pure gold; the French franc, .9097 grains. If as the old axiom tells us, "Things equal to the same thing are equal to each other," then the relation of the American dollar to the French franc (the "par of exchange" between them) must be as the relation of the weight of the gold in the dollar is to the weight of the gold in the franc. Dividing .9097 grains then by 23.22 grains, we find the result to be .03917. 3.917 American cents to the French franc, therefore, is found to be the "mint par of exchange" between the currency of the two countries.

Of little more than of academic interest when conditions are normal and the rate of exchange between two gold standard countries is moving along on an even keel, this question of "mint par" does of course assume a very great degree of practical importance when the balance of indebtedness swings heavily one way or the other and, the supply of bills having become inadequate, gold shipments become necessary to balance things up. What, after all, *but* the mint par determines the point in the rate of exchange at which gold will go out or come in? To buy gold at the mint price in one country and then send it abroad for credit of account at the mint price of some other country is, of course, a perfectly feasible way of establishing a foreign balance, but one which costs money. To the price originally paid for the gold, when it comes to figuring what it really cost to establish the balance abroad, there must be added all charges incident to the physical transfer of the gold to the other side— freight, insurance, loss of interest, etc., etc. If, then, when the transfer has been effected the newly created balance in francs or whatever the currency may be cannot be sold out for more dollars than it cost to put it over there, there is no profit in the transaction. What therefore determines whether or not specie shipments can profitably be made is the extent to which the price that the banker can realize for his drafts exceeds the "mint par" of exchange. When the excess equals the cost of shipping the gold, the exchange rate is said to be at the "gold export point." Any advance above that figure sufficient to give the banker even a moderate profit will start gold actually going out.

Cost of Shipping Gold

As to the actual cost of shipping gold, so many variable factors are involved that to attempt to state the figures even on a transaction between two specific points is to present a calculation certain to become obsolete within a very short time after it is made. Briefly, however, it may be said that the main items of expense are freight, marine insurance, Assay office charges and loss of interest. Of the first two of these it need only be said that they are subject to constant change; and, of the third, that the Assay office charge constitutes the charge made by the Government for the privilege of being able to buy bars officially assayed and certified. When it comes to having the gold received and credited in a foreign country, the fact of the bars being officially stamped, naturally greatly facilitates matters.

Where gold coin is used for export instead of bars there is of course no Assay office charge. Even so, however, bars are preferable by reason of the fact that bars are bought by actual weight, whereas coin has to be bought and paid for at its face value. If the coin available for export happens to be newly minted that makes little difference; but if, as is often the case, the coin has been in circulation and has suffered a certain amount of abrasion, the gold exporter finds himself paying for a certain amount of something he doesn't actually get. Coin abraded (worn down) beyond a certain point ($\frac{1}{2}$ of one percent), it is true, goes outside of the legal "limit of tolerance" and is barred from circulation; but even so, on coin still well within the limit, the loss in buying at its face value something that will be coldly credited by weight when it gets over to the other side, may be very considerable. By actual experimentation the Government has found that the average annual loss from abrasion is $1/60$ of one percent. If then the coin that the gold exporter gets from the Treasury has been in circulation for even as much as six years, the shortage in actual weight may amount to as much as $1/10$ of one percent. That, on a million-dollar shipment, would be a thousand dollars—enough, possibly, to wipe out the entire profit the shipper of the gold was trying to make. Quite a potential power then in the hands of a government desirous of hindering gold exports, this ability to hand out less than full weight coin. Clearly within the recollection of any number of foreign exchange bankers, a number of important occasions on which it has been invoked.

Loss of interest, the fourth main item of expense in connection with the shipment of specie, comes about by reason of the fact (1) that the banker who is doing the shipping has to buy and pay for the gold two days before he himself gets paid for the drafts he sells, (2) that two and sometimes more days elapse between the time the gold arrives at its destination abroad and the time it is actually credited to the American banker's account. As to the first of these two items, while it is a fact that the reimbursing drafts are sometimes sold at the same time that the gold is bought and paid for, in such cases a rebate of two days' interest is usually allowed to the purchasers of the bills. As to the other charge for interest following the arrival of the specie, that comes about by reason of the fact that the drafts, always rushed to their destination with all possible speed, are likely to be presented for payment a couple of days before the shipment of gold is received, verified and credited. Not at any time an excessively heavy charge, this four days' interest loss, at times when interest rates on both sides of the water happen to be high, can run into considerable money. At four percent, for instance, four days' interest on $1,000,000 is $444.

With the variable nature of the charges incident to the shipping of specie in mind, it will perhaps be a little plainer why it is impossible to present a hard-and-fast calculation as to the cost of shipping gold or to state definitely the point in the exchange rate at which gold will begin to flow out. If a rough estimate is wanted, it may be said that as between New York and any western European point the cost may be reckoned at ½ of one percent on the amount involved. In other words when any standard exchange rate rises ½% above its mint par the chances are that it stands very near to the point at which gold can profitably be exported.

Cost of Importing Gold

Turning now from consideration of exports to consideration of imports of gold, it will appear upon a moment's reflection that just as a rise in exchange above mint par equal to the cost of shipping gold will cause gold to go out, so a decline below mint par equal to the cost of importing gold will cause gold to come in. Essentially, we saw, the reason gold is sent out is that it has become cheaper to settle a debt abroad that way than by buying and sending over a draft. Similarly, quite, gold is brought in when a creditor here can realize more dollars by actually cashing his draft in the market on which it is drawn and bringing in the gold proceeds, than he can by following the usual procedure of selling the draft in his home market. Though here again, it is to be noted, it is not the actual owner of the draft who is likely to do the importing of the gold. Once more, as in the case of a gold export transaction, the intermediary foreign exchange banker comes into the picture. It is to him that the holder sells the draft on the foreign debtor and it is by him that the draft is sent abroad, turned into gold and the gold actually imported. Again, we see, it is a case of the specie transaction being handled by someone having the necessary facilities and willing, for the profit there is in it, to put up the necessary capital.

Theoretically, of course, what we think of as a gold import transaction is a gold export transaction on the other end, and, so, no different from the export transactions described in the preceding paragraphs. Practically, however, the case is different in that when we have payments to make on the other side we usually make them by buying and sending over bills of exchange, whereas, when we are owed money, we do not customarily wait for dollar drafts to be sent to us but are far more apt to draw sterling or franc or whatever the currency may be upon the buyers. Essentially, of course, the same thing, there *is* this one important point of difference: Under the first kind of arrangement the seller of the goods has to wait for his money till the drafts reach him. Under the second, the creditor here, able at once to draw a draft (though it may be at 60 or 90 days' sight) is in a position to sell that draft at once and, so, realize immediate payment.

To the subject under discussion the importance of this distinction lies in the fact that whereas in the case of a gold export transaction the intermediary banker does not have to use any of his own capital (except for a couple of days on each end), in the case of a gold import transaction he has to advance his own money from the time the gold is bought abroad until it is actually received and credited on this side. The creditor here, it has been explained, wants to get paid at once. Someone of course has to put up the money and that someone, where the debt is to be settled through the import of specie, is none other than the intermediary banker who steps in and in effect says to the creditor, "Here, let me have your draft and I'll cash it for you at once."

A gold import transaction thus differs from a gold export transaction in that in the former not only has some banker to be found who is willing to tie up his capital but that, in figuring the expense, a full ten days' interest has to be allowed for. Not an insuperable obstacle when conditions here are quiet and money rates are low, this circumstance that capital has to be tied up in the shipment and interest charged does, at times, work toward making it necessary for exchange to work well below the theoretical "good import" point before specie will actually begin to come in. A time, for example, when banking conditions are disturbed is likely to be a time when bankers will be hesitant about tying up a large sum of money merely in order to make the really very moderate profit usually to be made through the shipping out and the bringing in of specie. At a certain point, of course, assuming that conditions are not so bad that the banks are unwilling to tie up funds for *any* consideration, the margin of profit becomes so substantial that the banks *are* willing to put up the necessary funds and the decline in the exchange rate is thus brought to a halt. That, however, on numerous occasions in the past has proved to be only after rates have fallen to a point very considerably below the level at which specie imports might reasonably be expected to have been begun.

There is thus, it is to be noted, far more "play" in the amount by which exchange rates must drop below the "mint par" in order to make it sure that gold will come in than there is in the amount by which rates must rise above mint par in order to make it sure that gold will go out.

Gold as a Medium of Exchange

Leaving these questions of detail and turning to a broader and possibly more interesting aspect of the matter, to what extent, between two primary markets, does the shipment of gold actually figure in the settlement of debts and claims? At certain times, the record shows, to a very large extent; over a series of years to a far lesser degree, probably, than is generally imagined. These last few years, it is true, have been a time of upheaval here and abroad, of violent swings in exchange rates and consequent tremendous in and out shipments of gold. Such, however, is very far from being the normal relationship between two markets like New York and London, or London and Paris. So potent are the corrective forces which under normal conditions come into play the moment that any important exchange rate begins to move decidedly one way or the other, that the swing of rates is kept pretty well within bounds. Over a long series of years, for example, the entire annual movement of the pound sterling in the New York market will be found to have been only four or five cents. That, as the exchange market went prior to the disruptive conditions produced by the War, was considered a very great fluctuation indeed. What it amounted to, though,

actually, was a total variation of only about one percent in the value of the pound in terms of the American dollar.

One other thing in connection with this matter of
the relationship between the rate of exchange and
the movement of gold remains to be pointed out. That
is that by no means, especially in times like these, are
all inter-country gold shipments undertaken on a
strictly exchange basis—that is to say, that they necessarily represent a way of making a remittance, su-
perior, from a dollar-and-cents point of view, to the
use of bills of exchange. Gold, of course, in the general
scheme of things monetary, holds a place different
from even the best and soundest other forms of currency. Conditions not infrequently develop where the
banks at some important center determine that their
gold-holdings must be increased. If at such a time
these banks have substantial deposits abroad, even
though these deposits be in countries impregnably on
the gold basis, recall of such balances is likely to ensue.
Nor, under such circumstances, does it make any difference whether the exchange rate does or does not
happen to be at a point where recall of the funds could
be more advantageously effected through the sale of
bills of exchange than through importations of specie.
Gold, in the case we are discussing, is what is wanted
and it will be in the form of gold that the deposits will
be brought back. To sell bills would be only to take
the gold away from some neighbor bank, some bank
possibly quite as much or even more in need of it. If
the object is to build up that particular banking

community's gold holdings, the metal must come in from the outside. That, then, is what is done, regardless, as has been pointed out, of whether the prevailing exchange rate does or does not favor such operations. A definite object is to be accomplished, and the fact that the rate of exchange happens to be slightly above the point where gold would normally be imported, will by no means prevent its accomplishment.

Exchange between Gold and Non-Gold Countries

We have, in the foregoing discussion of exchange rates and the limits of their fluctuations been confined, necessarily, to countries on the gold standard with no existing restrictions on the free export and import of gold. A little further along and in its proper place the foreign exchange relationship of gold standard to non-gold-standard countries will be fully gone into; but, even so, our current discussion would be sadly incomplete were we to leave it without mention of a few of the more important things which limit the movement of exchange rates between countries which use gold and countries which do not.

Considering first the case of an exchange rate between a true gold standard country and a country with an inconvertible paper currency but with no restrictions on the export or import of gold, it will be found evident that while the points to which exchange can fall and rise are not limited by the same considerations as in the case of two gold standard countries, they are, nevertheless, very clearly defined. Essentially, as a matter of fact, the rules are not different. In both cases, it is the price of gold which governs. That price in a gold standard country being, as we have seen, the mint par; and, in a country whose paper is inconvertible and so which has no such thing as a mint par, the actual open market price at which gold like any other commodity is bought and sold.

England and the United States, at the time this is written in the above relationship, furnish the best possible example. For the time being at least, the owner of pounds sterling cannot, it is true, convert them into gold at the old fixed price of £3 17s 10½d. per ounce; but at a price, at whatever price gold happens in the open market to be selling, he can buy as much gold as he wants. The holder of pounds sterling, in other words, can buy gold just as he could before. The only difference is that whereas before England went off the gold standard he used to be able to buy gold at a fixed price, now he has to pay a premium for it.

It is this premium, of course, which fixes the limit of fluctuation in the rate of exchange. Just as in the days when both countries were on the gold basis the question used to be, "Can I realize more dollars by selling my drafts on London or by bringing in gold paid for at £3 17s 10½d. per ounce?" so now the question is, "Can I realize more dollars by selling my drafts on London or by bringing in gold paid for at the current open market rate?" Assuming that gold at some sort of a price is available (which in this case it is) it is still, as it always was, a cold matter of figuring. The alternative, just as it always was, is whether more dollars will be realized by selling the drafts in the home market for what they will bring or by sending them over, using the proceeds to buy gold at whatever the premium happens to be and then bringing that gold back for credit at the U. S. mint price. As to which course is followed, that, it is plain, is a question of the amount of the premium (in other words the price) which must be paid for the gold in the foreign market. Below the point at which it figures out better to buy and import gold, the rate of exchange will not go. Why should it? Below that point drafts will simply not be offered for sale.

Where Export Restrictions Exist

The above applies of course only to the rate of exchange between a gold standard country and an inconvertible paper country where there are no restrictions upon the free export and import of specie. Where such restrictions exist the case is naturally different and there are no limits to the extent to which rates of exchange can fall and rise. The matter, in that case, becomes purely one of supply and demand. If in the paper country there are debtors under the necessity of making payments in dollars, for instance, in New York, there is no possible way of making them except by going into the local market and finding someone willing to sell the necessary dollar draft at some sort of a price. Conversely, if the debtor happens to be in the gold country and no drafts on the paper country happen to be for sale, recourse cannot be had to the shipment of specie for the simple reason that in the kind of a country we are talking about gold cannot upon its arrival be converted into the local currency. Here again it is a case of the party with the remittance to make having to go out and pay whatever price is necessary for the kind of a draft he wants.

As between two such countries, however, it is to be noted that the balance of indebtedness will invariably be "against" the paper country to such a degree that the rate of exchange on the paper country will be found selling at a low and not a high price. A moment's reflection will show us why. For what reason, in the paper country, can a government embargo have been placed upon the export and import of gold except that the debts of that country to the outside world have come so largely to exceed its credits that whatever gold supply it possesses has come to be at the mercy of the people with whom it does business? Invariably where we find this condition of an embargo on specie shipments we find a case where the true balance between debits and credits has been running heavily in favor of the former and where the national currency, in consequence, is selling at a heavy discount in the outside markets.

Between Gold and Silver Countries

There having been considered the case of two gold countries, of a gold country and a paper country without restrictions on gold and of a gold country and a paper country *with* such restrictions, there remains finally to be considered only the case of a gold country and of a silver country. As between a gold standard market such as New York and a silver standard market such, for instance, as Shanghai, what determines the limits to which the rate of exchange can rise or fall?

Understanding of the matter will perhaps be facilitated by appreciation of the fact, at the very outset, that in a gold market like New York silver is simply a commodity like any other, and that in a silver market like Shanghai gold is simply a commodity like any other. Silver in New York is being constantly bought and sold at a changing price in terms of gold; while, in Shanghai the price of gold rises and falls in terms of silver. To the American banker, silver, and to the Chinese banker, gold, is just so much merchandise.

That being the case, it is evident that, in New York, the gold price of a draft on Shanghai payable in silver will rise and fall as the price of silver rises and falls. If at New York there is an increased demand for silver, the value of a draft payable in silver will of course tend to increase. If on the other hand there is in New York an over supply of silver and the price of silver declines, it is plain that less gold dollars will be paid for a draft calling for payment in silver.

Similarly, of course, with regard to the price in the Far East of drafts on New York payable in gold. If Shanghai has been buying heavily in the western markets and drafts payable in gold with which to make remittances are in heavy demand, the price of those drafts, naturally, in terms of silver, will tend to advance. More of the local silver currency, in other words, will be needed to buy a gold draft on America for the same amount.

What then in a gold country limits the rise and fall in the rate of exchange on a silver country? The same thing exactly as was found to limit the rate on a country with an inconvertible paper currency but without restrictions on the import and export of gold. In that case, as we saw, it was the open-market price of gold which governed the rate of exchange. In the case of a silver using country, it is the price of silver. New York, we will say, on account of heavy importations of silk not balanced by corresponding exports of our own products, is heavily indebted to Hongkong or Shanghai. Drafts on the Far East payable in silver come into demand and the price rises sharply. How far can the rate rise? To that point and only to that point, it is plain, where the American banker or importer with a remittance to make figures that he can make it more cheaply by buying and sending a draft than by buying and sending silver. The moment it costs materially more to use drafts as a form of remittance, silver will begin to go out and the demand for drafts will come to an end.

Attempt has been made in the preceding paragraphs to show how, when the balance of indebtedness between two countries swings too heavily one way or the other, settlement of debts and claims is made through the medium of shipments of specie. The "mint parity" of the currencies of gold standard countries was then explained and the figures in connection with the shipment of gold were gone into in some detail. The broad view of the part actually played by specie shipments in the settlement of inter-country debts and claims was then considered, special emphasis being placed on those specie transactions not undertaken for profit but in order to satisfy an insistent need for gold. Finally there were considered the limits on the movement of exchange rates between gold standard and non-gold standard countries, both those having non-convertible paper currencies with and without restrictions on gold, and those on a straight silver basis.

CHAPTER V

THE INTERRELATION OF
EXCHANGE RATES

WITH the world's main exchange markets closely connected and in constant communication, it is plain that a definite relationship between the principal rates of exchange must at all time exist. With New York and Paris, for example, constantly on the telephone, it is evident that the price of pounds sterling in Paris cannot move materially up or down without the price of pounds sterling in New York being affected. Transfer of funds by cable between points like New York and Paris can be so easily and rapidly made that, to all practical purposes, these markets are as one. No more possible is it for the rate for pounds to move importantly in Paris without affecting the rate for pounds in New York than it is for the price of cotton in New York to move importantly without affecting the price of cotton in Liverpool.

"Parity" of Exchange Rates

We shall perhaps make the greatest progress in our initial attack upon this problem of the interrelation of foreign exchange rates if we take three points, assume arbitrarily that at some given time certain definite rates of exchange exist between them, and then endeavor to follow what necessarily happens when in any of these rates there takes place any material change. The three points we had perhaps best take are New York, Paris and London. The rates we shall assume (this for the sole purpose, through the absence of decimals and fractions, of making the computation as understandable as possible) will be: Price of pounds sterling in New York, \$3.60 per pound; price of pounds sterling in Paris, 90 francs per pound; price of francs in New York, 4 cents per franc.

The above combination of rates, a moment's figuring will show, represents that condition of affairs referred to in most writings on foreign exchange as "triangular parity." Sand in the gears of most explanations of the interrelation of exchange rates, this frightening term "triangular parity" means really nothing less or more than that as between the three markets the rates given above are in perfect balance. At New York the price of the draft on London is \$3.60 per pound, and the price of the draft on Paris (at which point, at the time, drafts on London can be bought at 90 francs per pound) is four cents per franc. In other words, to the American banker the cost of the pound, under the above conditions is \$3.60 whether he buys that pound in New York or in Paris. From the angle of the Paris banker, the purchase of a pound in London, where that pound can be used to buy \$3.60 in New York, will cost 90 francs—which is just exactly what it would cost the Paris banker to buy a draft for \$3.60 direct on New York. In London, thirdly, the cost of a draft for \$3.60 on New York, where the \$3.60 can be used to buy 90 francs, is one pound—exactly what he would have had to pay for 90 francs drawn direct on Paris.

It seldom if ever happens, of course, that between any three given points rates of exchange are on the perfect parity given above. It is a fact, however, that at no time can the combination of rates get very far away from parity. Material movement of any one of three rates is bound immediately to affect both the others and to bring them into line.

How One Rate Affects Another

Let us suppose, to continue our illustration with the rates used above, that for some given reason a heavy selling movement of pounds sets in in Paris. The banks there, we will say, desirous of decreasing the sterling balances they are carrying with their correspondents in London, begin offering sterling drafts for sale. The price of such drafts then, which when the selling movement began stood at 90 francs per pound, declines perhaps to a point where the pound can be bought for 89 francs. "Ho, ho," says the banker in New York, "here's my chance to buy some pounds in Paris and to sell them out here for more than they cost me. With the franc here at four cents and the pound in Paris at 89 francs, I can now 'lay down' pounds in London at $3.56. With drafts on London here at $3.60 I can immediately sell out those pounds at a profit of four cents each." [Author's note: The figures given, like the rates used, are to be regarded as purely illustrative and not as representing actual conditions.]

But wait a moment, just what is going to be the effect of what this profit-seeking banker and many others like him are going to do? They are, in the first place, in order to pay for the pounds they are buying in Paris, going to buy franc drafts on Paris. That is going to make the rate on Paris go up. They are, in the second place, in order to cash in, going to sell sterling drafts on London. That is going to make the rate on London go down. All of which, of course, is going to tend to narrow the profit on the transaction. To keep on narrowing it, in fact, until there is nothing worth while left for the banker to go for, and, so, the buying and selling comes to an end of its own momentum. The rates, in other words, have come back into line; or, if the language of the cambist is preferred, have again approximated "triangular parity."

There has been shown, in the above, how a decline in the price of pounds in Paris will tend, at New York, to raise the rate for francs and to lower the price of sterling. We might, if we wished, go on, and, first taking London and then New York, show how a rise or fall in exchange rates at those points is bound to affect rates between the other two cities. That, however, is probably unnecessary. If the theory of the thing as exemplified by the case actually given is clearly understood, there can be no possible difficulty in figuring what kind of effect a change in any given rate is going to have on the two others. Cheaper pounds in Paris mean cheaper pounds in New York or any other center closely connected with Paris. Dearer francs in New York mean dearer francs in London, etc., etc.

The above presupposes, of course, that we are dealing with markets of the first magnitude, closely in touch with each other and constantly engaged in reciprocal transactions of great size. Where one of the three points is of lesser importance and not constantly dealing on a large scale with the two others, the principles set forth can hardly be expected to hold. A decline in the price of sterling at Buenos Aires, for example, would hardly be sufficient to exert much of an influence on the price of sterling in New York. If the decline in sterling at Buenos Aires amounted to much there would undoubtedly be a certain amount of buying from New York; but, the rate between New York and Buenos Aires being sensitive as it is, the chances are that it would quickly rise to a point making unprofitable the purchase of pounds sterling at that point. As to the effect on the sterling rate in New York of the sale of whatever pounds happened to be purchased in Buenos Aires, the strong probability is that the market here would absorb such selling without its being felt at all.

Sensitiveness of Rates

We come then on an important principle governing this interrelation of exchange rates and that is that while the rise or fall of any rate will make itself felt on the others, it will make itself felt first and most on the rate between the two points in the triangle having the least amount of financial intercourse. In the case mentioned above of New York, London and Buenos Aires, that rate was of course the New York-Buenos Aires one, our foreign exchange relations with that center being of nowhere near as much importance as are those with London. It was at that point that the corrective was applied and the adjustment made which brought the three rates back to "triangular parity."

As among the rates prevailing between the three great financial centers of the world, London, Paris and New York, the most sensitive to changes in the others is the franc rate between New York and Paris and the one least sensitive the sterling rate between London and New York. By that it is not at all meant that the fluctuations in the franc rate are more than the fluctuations in the sterling rate, the exact opposite indeed being the case. What is meant is that the volume of financial interchange between New York and Paris is so much less than the volume of financial interchange between New York and London, that the incidence of a suddenly increased buying or selling movement has a much greater and more immediately apparent effect on the market for francs than on the market for pounds. It is after all very much as in the case of the market for a widely held and actively traded-in stock like United States Steel and the market for some other stock, Union Pacific for example, also widely held but not nearly so actively traded in. Just as a selling order for several thousand shares of Steel is under normal conditions absorbed with little effect on the price, while in the case of Union Pacific the execution of a sell order for a similar amount of stock can usually be accomplished only at a material concession, so, in the market for pounds sterling a volume of selling or buying can usually be absorbed without difficulty which in the market for francs would give rates a serious jolt in one direction or the other.

The perfectly good reason why this is so is not only because New York does a far larger volume of business with London than with Paris, but because, in spite of everything that has happened, in spite even of Britain's having been temporarily forced off the gold basis, London remains the point through which by far the greatest proportion of the world's import and export transactions of merchandise are cleared. To this day and in spite of Paris having been able to remain on the gold basis where London has not, it is in London and not in Paris that the great bulk of Continental Europe's purchases from and sales to South America and the Near and Far East are settled and paid for. Even in our own case, allowing for all the inroads we have made on London's traditional position as the world's commercial clearing house, it is a fact that a very large proportion of the trade carried on by the United States with the outside world is financed not by means of credits opened in New York in dollars but by credits opened in London in pounds. The custom of centuries is not lightly to be changed. Great as has been the increase in the prestige of the dollar in world trade, there are innumerable merchants in every part of the world who, when they sell something in the United States, demand that their payment be made not in dollars in New York but in the pounds sterling in London.

When to the above is added the fact—the two of course have a great deal to do with each other—that the discount market in London remains by far the greatest reservoir of liquid capital in the world available for the pre-payment of obligations not yet due, it becomes very evident why it is that the volume of foreign exchange transactions in sterling is hugely in excess of the volume in any other currency under the sun. It becomes evident why it is that of the rates between New York, Paris and London it is the New York-London sterling rate which is by all odds the most important and the least liable to be affected by exchange fluctuations taking place elsewhere.

Influences from the Outside

In our above discussion of the interrelation of exchange rates we assumed that, at some important point like Paris, there was a sharp change in rates caused by local market conditions of one sort or another, and then endeavored to trace the effect on rates between the other two points in the triangle. What we have now to consider is what happens not when some given exchange rate is affected by conditions prevailing within that market but, rather, what happens when some given exchange rate is subjected to heavy selling or buying from some other point. Just as this is written, for example, Paris, figuring that the rate for pounds sterling at New York is likely to advance, has been buying sterling on a tremendous scale in New York, with the result that sterling has been driven upward by as much as ten cents per pound in the course of a single day. How, we have now to inquire, are the other rates affected by such a condition of things?

To take the case mentioned above: If Paris is buying pounds in New York, Paris, it is evident, must have dollars to do its purchasing with. If we assume that

Paris already has a sufficient amount of dollars to its credit in New York, the effect on the New York-Paris franc rate will be negligible. Such, however, is not likely to be the case. A speculative buying movement in sterling such as we are speaking about is far more likely to originate in speculative quarters than among large banks having large deposits of dollars here. Those speculators, then, or "operators," or whatever you choose to call them, are under the necessity of sending dollars to New York with which to make their purchases of sterling. That means that either the "operators" in France will have to buy dollar drafts or dollar cables in the Paris market and send them to New York or else they will have to direct their correspondents in New York to draw upon them in francs. The result will of course, as we have seen, be exactly the same: The franc will decline in relation to the dollar, or as it may perhaps be more understandably stated, the exchange rate on Paris will go down in New York.

What will be the effect on the other rate, that between London and Paris? Clearly that, in London, the price of francs will go down. With London able to buy more dollars in New York with each pound, and with those dollars in New York buying more francs, it is plain that London will not be slow to take advantage of the opportunity to (1) buy dollar drafts on New York, (2) use them to buy franc drafts on Paris, (3) draw franc drafts on Paris in order to bring home the proceeds—and, incidentally, the bacon. The effect of which drawing and offering of franc drafts in London will be, of course, to make that rate go down.

The Theory of "Arbitrage"

London, Paris and New York have been used in the above illustrations. Any other points having close foreign exchange relationships with one another might just as well have been taken. Operations such as have been touched on, as a matter of fact, are by no means limited to three centers, it being plainly possible to make a remittance from New York, for instance, to Paris, by way not only of one but of two or even three intervening markets. Such operations, however, constitute a refinement of exchange dealings of far more interest to the foreign exchange manager than to the business man or student interested rather in gaining a grasp of the subject as a whole. To attempt further to multiply instances would, in all probability, be simply to bring confusion into the matter. Knowing the principle on which the thing works, it is perfectly simple to take any given set of conditions and, from them, to work out the required result.

That, as a matter of fact, is what is being done every hour of every day in the foreign exchange department of every bank having important foreign connections. "Parity sheets" worked out by each bank to suit its individual requirements do, it is a fact, work to facilitate rapid calculation; but what really happens is that each manager, alert and everlastingly informed as to what changes in rates are going on elsewhere, is constantly figuring the possibility of making these "arbitrage" transactions. What is apparently only a slight change in the exchange rate between two distant markets may be quite sufficient to start the arbitrageur here or in London selling or buying some related currency at some entirely different point. The amounts dealt in by the banks, it must be remembered, are very large, so that even the smallest of rate fluctuations run into money. On a million francs, for example (roughly $40,000 in our money), a fluctuation of only five one-thousandths of a cent per franc means a difference of fifty dollars. Were there any credit risk or tie-up of funds involved, profits at such a rate would not perhaps be interesting. Where, however, the whole operation involves merely the sending of a cable or two to a market with which one is in constant touch; and where within an hour or so after he goes into the operation the banker has completed it and got back his money, he will be found ready to work for a very small profit indeed.

Indirect Settlements

What makes possible, it may well at this point be asked, all this swapping around of drafts (or cables) between markets? How is it that the seller can always find a buyer and vice versa? As between markets like New York, London and Paris it is understandable of course that there should be in progress a constant settlement of debts and claims; but how about some of these other and lesser markets? How is it, for example, that in the case we mentioned of a New York arbitrageur wanting to buy a cable on Buenos Aires in order there to buy a cable on London, there is always somebody ready to sell it to him?

The answer is to be found in the fact, previously stated, that settlements for exports and imports are not apt to be made directly between points of lesser importance, but are far more likely to be cleared through some pivotal center such as London or Amsterdam. A Czecho-Slovakian exporter of toys, for example, who has made a shipment to Argentina, would in all probability receive his payment not in the form of crowns payable in Prague but of pounds sterling payable in London. To all parties concerned such an arrangement would be more convenient. The importer in Buenos Aires will find no difficulty in buying a sterling draft with which to make his payment, whereas, if he had to buy a draft on Prague payable in crowns, he might encounter considerable difficulty in so doing. The Czecho-Slovakian exporter, on the other hand, is just as well off receiving his payment in pounds as in his own currency. To get his crowns, all he has to do is to draw a sterling draft on the balance which has been established for him in London. All of which, of course, is only another way of saying that it is by way of London, instead of directly, that he gets paid.

The above illustration is not brought in to begin a discussion of how exports or imports are paid for, but merely to show how, all over the world, sterling bills on London (and to an important though lesser degree, franc bills on Paris, guilder bills on Amsterdam, dollar bills on New York) are brought into supply and demand. This, then, is the reason why the arbitrageur in a standard currency finds no difficulty in dealing with these points of lesser importance. Their commercial relationships may, it is true, be with each other, but their financial relationships are with some focal point. The shellac that Ceylon produces may be used to smooth a surface in Sweden, but the outcome of the sale of that shellac will be that in Colombo someone will have a sterling bill to sell and that in Stockholm someone will have a sterling bill to buy.

In concluding our discussion of the interrelation of foreign exchange rates too much emphasis can hardly be laid on the fact that, connected as they are, New York, Paris, London and the world's other principal financial centers constitute what is really one great financial market. Rapid as is the communication afforded by the submarine cable, the development of the trans-oceanic telephone has during the past few years made communication even more rapid and convenient. In the seclusion of his office on Wall or Lombard Street, the foreign exchange manager picks up the receiver of his telephone and in a moment is in full possession of information as to what is going on not only in the market with which he is in direct communication but in all other markets in which he may be interested. Naturally, under such circumstances, it is impossible for any important exchange rate to move without the others being affected.

CHAPTER VI

NEW YORK—THE AMERICAN FOREIGN EXCHANGE AND DISCOUNT MARKET

In our necessarily more or less academic discussion in the preceding chapter of the interrelation of rates, frequent mention has been made of "buying by New York," "selling by London," etc., etc. It will be well now, perhaps, to examine a little more closely into the nature of these markets. Who in New York, for example, does the buying and selling, and what is the physical method of fixing the rates at which bills of exchange are actually bought and sold? Without departing from our intention, in other words, of making this book a discussion of fundamental principles rather than a manual of foreign exchange practice, may it not be advisable, perhaps, to get more down to cases and to tie in some of these principles we have been discussing with the way things are actually done?

New York the Focal Point

Much that is to follow will be made clearer and more understandable if we appreciate, at the very outset, that, so far as dealings in foreign exchange are concerned, New York is the focal point of the entire country. Chicago, Pittsburgh and other big cities, it is true, have their important banks with their own correspondents abroad, with whom their direct dealings often run into large volume. By that, however, there is not in the least altered the fact that, so far as the transactions in foreign exchange of the vast majority of banks throughout the country are concerned, it is in and through New York that these transactions are actually consummated. New Orleans or Chicago can, of course, and do, draw direct on Manchester or Liverpool; but when it comes to the disposing of these bills in the most advantageous way possible, it will be in the great competitive market at New York that that will actually be done.

Take, for example, points like Minneapolis or St. Louis where large exports of grain and other food products originate, or points like Galveston and New Orleans from which a very considerable proportion of the cotton crop is shipped abroad—from what source, at such centers, could there originate a demand for foreign exchange sufficient to absorb the tremendous volume of bills created when cotton and grain shipments get fully under way? From no possible source whatever. Make the fullest estimate of the maximum demand for bankers' bills which can ever originate at these interior points and we shall still find it entirely inadequate to take care of the supply. In one way and in one way only can these export bills be disposed of and that is by selling them in that market upon which converges the whole country's demand for the means of making foreign remittances. In other words, in New York.

What happens then is that exporters and importers all over the country as well as their local banks establish and maintain close connections in New York for the handling of their foreign exchange business. Through these connections they keep constantly in touch with the fluctuation in rates. How otherwise would it be possible, for example, for a milling concern in Minneapolis to make sales of flour to a foreign buyer—the price quoted being, as it is, governed largely by the rate of exchange which the exporter receives for his bills? Constantly then, at interior points, the man who is selling in England and the man who is buying in France have got to keep themselves informed as to the movement of exchange rates in New York. They, that is to say, or their local banks. A very large volume of exchange, of course, is handled for the interior exporter or importer by his bank in his home city. In many cases this, indeed, is the preferable method. In the first place, the local bank is usually able to maintain a closer and more satisfactory contact with New York. In the second place, the importer's or exporter's home bank, being of course more familiar with the nature of his business and the strength of his credit, is able to quote him closer rates that he would be able to get if he had to do his own buying and selling in the New York market.

The fact that hundreds of banks throughout the country have arrangements with the big foreign exchange banks in New York whereby they (the interior banks) are able to draw direct upon the European correspondents of the New York banks, alters the above situation not at all. A firm in Kansas City we will say, has a payment to make in sterling in Leeds or Birmingham. The necessary draft can, to be sure, be bought right in Kansas City. But the

Kansas City bank which draws it—without, of course, itself carrying any balance in London—to whom must the Kansas City bank send the necessary "cover" in dollars? To some bank in New York. And where, after all, is the rate of exchange determined which fixes what the exact amount of "cover" due the New York bank shall be? In the New York foreign exchange market. Analyze the operation a little and all it turns out to be is a method by which the New York foreign exchange bank sells a draft on London to its interior correspondent. The fact that it is the interior bank and not the New York bank which actually draws the draft makes no essential difference. The bill, after all, is drawn against the New York bank's foreign balance and it is the New York bank which has got to take care of the draft whether it happens to be drawn by the New York bank itself or by some interior correspondent which has been authorized so to draw.

N. Y. Exchange Market—the Banks

Of what sort of institutions and firms in New York is this frequently referred to "exchange market" constituted?

First, the large incorporated banks of deposit, national and state, practically all of which have to-day well established foreign departments. Next, the great international banking houses, private partnerships most of them. Next, the investment and brokerage houses with a business largely domestic but with foreign connections sufficient at times to put them in the market as buyers and sellers of bills on a substantial scale. Finally the inevitable middle men, the foreign exchange "brokers."

Taking first the institutional banks, we find here a class of dealers in foreign exchange who, during the past two decades, have come to overshadow all the others in importance and in the scope of their operations. Far less of a factor at the beginning of the present century than were the privately owned banking houses, these institutions, especially since the War, have built up their foreign departments to a point where it can safely be said that by them there it today being handled the great bulk of the country's foreign exchange business. Employing enormous amounts of capital, directed by the best procurable brains, equipped with a highly trained personnel running in many cases into the hundreds and, above all, with their own branches in foreign cities, these banks are in a position to take advantage of every possible opportunity offered in foreign exchange. In addition to all of which, of course, they enjoy the very great advantage of having literally thousands of correspondent banks scattered all over the country who, as previously described, feed them business both on the buying and selling side.

The Private Banking Houses

Of first importance, too, of course, are the privately owned international banking houses. Identified from the very beginning with this business of foreign exchange and with connections built up here and abroad during the course of the better part of a century, these firms occupy a position from which not even the phenomenal growth of "institutionalized" foreign exchange banking has been able to dislodge them. If today the volume of their business relative to the whole is not as great as it used to be, that is not because of anything that has been taken away from them but simply because of the huge additional volume of business developed by the national and state banks. Though, at that, the fact must not be overlooked that to a large extent the foreign exchange operations of these firms have always originated from European-American security transactions—the placing of American securities in Europe, and vice-versa—a form of business which in recent years has shown a very great falling off.

The same thing is true and to an even greater extent with regard to the investment and brokerage houses whose foreign security business necessitates the maintenance of a foreign exchange department. Of great importance during the palmy days of foreign bond financing here and of active European participation in the American stock market, and at times originating and absorbing large amounts of exchange, the foreign departments of these firms are under present circumstances of considerably less account. Primarily, be it remembered, these foreign departments were established and maintained for the facilitation of the firm's foreign security business rather than for the making of profits out of foreign exchange operations in general. Now, therefore, that Europe has so largely been baled out of her holdings of "Americans" and that inter-country stock and bond transactions have fallen to so low a point, many if not most of these investment house foreign exchange departments are functioning at a greatly reduced pace. Some indeed have already been discontinued altogether—to be resurrected, however, no doubt, when the old time international security relations are once more resumed.

The Foreign Exchange Broker

Providing a direct means of contact between the above classes of dealers in bills, and also functioning as the connecting link between many buyers and sellers of exchange located in the interior, and New York, are the foreign exchange "brokers." Here, as in the case of most active markets, we have the middleman. Of lowly or exalted estate according as the exchange market is quiet or excited, decried by some but used by all, the foreign exchange broker continues, as he has always been, a vital cog in the foreign exchange machine. With all the improvement in communication methods which has taken place, with all the connecting telephones and the private wires, the broker remains and always will remain, for the simple reason that he furnishes the human element so indispensable in the bringing together of the man who has something to buy and the man who has something to sell.

For reasons of their own, as a matter of fact, the big buyers and sellers of exchange decidedly prefer to deal through brokers. Located along Wall and Pine Streets and Lower Broadway almost within a stone's throw of each other, one might think that these banks and bankers would prefer to deal direct with one another, but such is very far from being the case. It is, after all, a most tremendously competitive business, with each foreign exchange manager ever watchful of the interests of his own institution. And, just as many operators in stocks who are members of the Stock Exchange never go on the Floor, preferring to entrust the execution of their buying orders and selling to reliable agents, so these foreign exchange operators work through brokers who have been successful in winning their confidence.

There is, of course, in New York, no central point where exchange is bought and sold, no one place where brokers meet as they do when trading in stocks. Dealings are conducted entirely on an "over-the-counter" basis, which means, most of the time, by telephone. No longer, to any degree, as in former times, do the brokers circulate personally among the banks. The broker's office to-day is equipped with a battery of telephones, private wires running into the offices of most of the big buyers and sellers of exchange. Occasionally, as in the old days, a broker will be called in by a bank and entrusted with some buying and selling commission, but it is over the wires that most of the business is actually done.

The Commercial Bill Broker

In addition to those who specialize in thus contacting the banks, there is another class of foreign exchange brokers interested mainly in handling the commercial bills which originate all over the country. To a certain extent this business, as we have seen, has come to be handled by the interior banks. There still remain, however, many exporting firms in various parts of the country who figure that they can dispose of their bills more advantageously through the agency of some broker regularly representing them in the New York market, than in any other way. In which method, indeed, there are many important advantages. Substantial as the exporter in the interior may be and considerable as may be the volume of the bills he originates, it is a fact that some competent broker representing him right along in New York is in a better position to find just who at any given time is going to be willing to pay him the highest price for his bills than is the local bank back home. Such-and-such a bank here in New York is to-day buying such-and-such a type of bill and glad to get them—who, more than the foreign exchange broker right on the ground, is in a position to know what is currently what about such matters? The services of such a broker cost money, of course; but, particularly in the case of commercial bills, the cost is one which the traffic will bear. A commercial bill drawn, for instance, against a shipment of machinery does not, like a bill drawn by a bank on a bank, command at any given time a definitely ascertainable price. Out of what he saves by having the bill properly "shopped" in New York as against just having it sold perhaps to the first bank which happens to make an offer, the exporter can well afford to pay his broker in New York a substantial commission. Also, the banks who buy commercial bills come to know the brokers who handle the type of paper they want, which means that the broker is often put in a position to wire his client a bid with which the client would not possibly otherwise come in contact.

Uniformity of Rates

This foreign exchange "market" in New York is thus, we see, made up of a number of different elements—of the big producers and users of exchange here in the city, of the makers and buyers of bills all over the country, and of the brokers who furnish the liaison between them. How is it that with so many different elements and forces at work and with no one point at which the buying and selling is centralized, there can be any uniformity in quotations? How is it that as between any two given banks, the price on a trade at any particular time will not differ materially from the price on a trade between any other two banks?

The answer is that so perfect is the system of intercommunication between the various parties interested in what is going on, that the whole thing really works as one big market. The wires out of a properly equipped foreign exchange brokerage house, remember, reach not one or two but dozens of large buyers and sellers of exchange. From the end of his wire system, therefore, the broker is in a position to tell pretty well what is going on. His lights flash and, on several of his wires, offerings of exchange begin to come in. On another wire a bid comes in which, perhaps, enables him to consummate a trade. That price for the moment at least is established. Will the next trade be at a higher or lower figure? That depends, of course, upon the balance between bids and offers. Gradually as the weight of buying orders or selling orders predominates, the price at which the business is done is forced up or down. And always, so far as any standard class of bills is concerned, at a remarkably uniform price. The transactions, it is true, take place in a number of different banking and exchange brokerage offices, but all these, we have seen, are connected by private telephone, either directly, or by reason of the fact that the brokers' wires run into the same banks. The making of the actual trades is reported on no official sheet, but, with the interested parties interconnected as they are, whatever is happening in any one part of the market is at once pretty well known in every other part. Though at that, of course, there *are* times of fluctuation in rates so violent that trades may be synchronously made at varying quotations. That, however, is no different from what necessarily happens in any excited market, on the floor of the New York Stock Exchange or anywhere else. Quickly enough these discrepancies tend to smooth themselves out. With so many brokers bent on executing the orders with which they have been entrusted and with so many dealers keenly watching for every possibility to buy at one price and sell at another, the chance for a continued simultaneous difference in quoted prices is reduced to practically nothing.

One other point about this matter of the contact between the big buyers and sellers of exchange remains to be mentioned and that is the fact that the function of the man who acts as the go-between is sometimes that of dealer and sometimes that of broker. Never, of course, supposed to act as principal and as agent at the same time, the foreign exchange "broker" as he is loosely called, has, naturally, the right, under any given set of circumstances, to determine in which one of the two ways he prefers to operate. Under certain conditions he may feel that it is safest and best for him to confine himself strictly to a commission business, the comparative smallness of his possible earning being made up for by the fact that he is taking no risk. Under other conditions he may *want* to take the risk of a rise or a fall in rates with the of course much greater possible profits which accrue to a principal who is right in his market estimates. Acting as a broker, he can make his currently fixed commission of "⅛"—the difference, for example, between $3.75 and 3.75125 per pound sterling —the princely sum of $12.50 on £10,000. Acting as a principal, he can of course, in a moving market, if he happens to catch it right, make many times that amount. With the sterling market moving, as it frequently does, several cents per pound in a day, it is nothing unusual for a dealer, and this without using any capital at that, to buy sterling from a bank for his own account at, say, $3.80, hold off for half an hour or so and then sell it to some other bank at $3.81 or $3.82. One cent or two cents on each of, say, ten thousand pounds is, naturally, an entirely different proposition from the "⅛" (and there is talk as this is written of cutting that in half) which can be earned in a straight brokerage trade.

The New York Discount Market

So much then for the market in which drafts on foreign countries are bought and sold. How now about

the market in which a time bill drawn against a shipment of merchandise, after it has been sent across the
water and presented to the drawee and "accepted,"
passes from hand to hand? This, too, as we shall find,
is a vastly important part of the foreign exchange
market. Metamorphosed now from a plain "long bill
with documents attached" into a "bank acceptance,"
here is something which has come to figure vitally in
the whole operation of our modern banking system.
What the market conditions happen to be for the
buying and selling, in other words for the "discounting" of such bills, has a tremendous influence on the
rate of exchange. In our study of what affects exchange rates then, it will pay us to look carefully into
at least that part of the "discount market" in which
acceptances, originating in the course of inter-country
trade, are bought and sold.

The discount market in New York is, of course, of
comparatively recent origin and, in more senses than
one, is just beginning to approach its majority. Prior
to the establishment of the Federal Reserve System
in 1914 the banks were not allowed to "accept" time
drafts, which meant, naturally, that anything in the
nature of a discount market in the sense at least in
which that term is understood abroad, was out of the
question. The discount market such as it is, then,
has been developed during the course of the past
eighteen years. During the course of the past ten or
twelve years, it might perhaps better be said; for it
was not until the war had been over for at least a
couple of years that a discount market along anything
like its current lines really came into existence.

A New Phase

The New York discount market then, it will appear, is a really new phase of American banking, which explains, perhaps, some of the difficulties under which it finds itself constantly laboring. There was not, of course, when the Reserve System sprang full-panoplied from the brow of Senator Glass and its other progenitors, any large body of bankers in the country trained in acceptance banking, or, indeed, even reasonably familiar with the conduct of a market in bank acceptances. All that had to be learned, and not a little of it by bitter experience. Furthermore the establishment of a discount market was at the beginning regarded as something of an experiment; so that, in their desire to play safe, the framers of the law hedged it about with all possible restrictions and regulations. We need a discount market, it was felt, but this is all very new to us and we had best proceed with extreme caution at the beginning. A wise policy under the circumstances, no doubt, but one which gave the new market a slow start in its competition with the old-established discount markets in London and on the Continent.

Particularly so in view of the fact that the establishment of a discount market where there has never been one before is not merely a matter of providing the necessary facilities but means, as well, that the outside world has got to be persuaded to take advantage of those facilities. To pass a law making it legal for a bank to "accept" a three months' draft is one thing. To make a shipper of goods to the U. S. A. think that he wants to draw that kind of a draft when all his life he has been accustomed to drawing a different kind of a draft on a different place, is something entirely different. Greatly as we ourselves esteem the dollar, there were and still are found to be parts of the world in which it is not so highly esteemed. Draw drafts in dollars on New York?—said the shippers of rubber and jute and tea in far-off places; why should we do that and who is going to take these drafts off our hands after we do draw them? If you want us to ship you our produce, arrange it, as you have always done, so that we can draw 90-day bills on London for which, out here, there is always a good demand. You want us, instead to draw in dollars on New York? How are we to know that if we do so we are going to be able to get some one here in this market to buy these drafts from us at a close rate of exchange? How, in other words, are we to be sure of immediate payment for the goods we are shipping to you?

Establishing the Market

The establishment of a discount market in New York for foreign acceptances was thus, it will be seen, not so easy a proposition. There was first this lack of familiarity with American drafts on the part of shippers, above referred to. There was secondly the fact that bankers out in the East and in Africa and in South America, not being quite sure of what kind of a discount market would really exist in New York for bills of this sort, were a little loath to buy them from their clients. They would be very glad, these bankers at first told the tea and jute and rubber shippers, to take their bills on New York "for collection," in other words, to send the bills to New York, collect on them and then pay the shippers. That, however, suited the shippers not at all. The first principle of their business, they said, was to get paid at the time the goods were shipped. A sterling bill on London would make that possible. A dollar draft on New York would not.

The difficulties attending the establishment of the discount market in its early days are thus emphasized because only by an understanding of these facts will we appreciate why it took so long to get the market started and why, even now, several years later, the market still at times creaks badly in its operation. The trouble, be it noted, lay by no means entirely with the foreign shippers who were hesitant about drawing on New York, and the foreign bankers who were hesitant about taking drafts off their hands on a cash basis. We ourselves, to no little extent, were also to blame. The law, it is true, now allowed the banks to "accept" drafts drawn on them from abroad; but the banks—with the exception perhaps of a dozen large institutions—not being too familiar with the practice relating to commercial acceptances, were none too eager to allow themselves to be drawn on. Then, when that feeling was finally overcome and time drafts on New York in considerable volume did begin to come through, it soon became apparent that unfamiliarity with acceptances of this class on the part of our bankers in general was very greatly restricting the number of buyers and "discounters" of such paper. There were times, indeed, in the early stages of the market, when the Federal Reserve Bank itself was about the only dependable buyer of these accepted foreign bills.

The whole idea of a really broad and satisfactory discount market, of course, presupposes the existence of a large body of participants, banks mostly, willing and ready at all times both to buy and sell bills in large amount. A few big institutions willing at times to buy bills for the purpose of holding them to maturity cannot and do not constitute a real discount market. Vital to such a condition is a large number of institutional and other buyers of bills willing to take them on not only at those occasional times when they happen to have no other use for their loanable funds, but always carrying in portfolio an amount of such paper which increases and decreases as conditions dictate. To figure never to buy a bill except for the purpose of holding it through to maturity, to consider it an admission of weakness ever to sell or re-discount a batch of bills before they come due—acting along those lines no group of banks would ever get very far with the establishment of a discount market. A market to be a market has got to have sellers as well as buyers. No bill-dealing business of any importance could be established and run in a market in which the activity was sporadic and always preponderantly on the buying side.

The Discount Market Finally Established

Considerable, however, as were the difficulties under which the American discount market was originally established, they have now to a large extent been overcome, and there exists in New York City today a broad and active market in which acceptances originating from foreign commerce are bought and sold. There are not yet in New York, as there are in London, it is true, a large number of substantial "discount houses" operating in the bill market, and the number of private investors who realize the advantages of investing surplus funds in bills is still comparatively small. The banks more and more, however, are going in for bills and, what is of even greater importance, are losing the feeling that a bill once purchased must positively be held to maturity. Mr. Smith of the Third National Bank of Jonesville no longer boasts that *his* institution has never borrowed and never will borrow a dollar from the local Federal Reserve Bank. If tax money or some other temporary deposit comes into his bank in large amount these days, he is quite likely to call up New York and have his correspondent buy acceptances with the extra money. Then, when things tighten up again and he needs money for his regular customers, he is quite as likely to order the bills sold or to send them for rediscount to the Reserve. The great advantages of the bill market as a place for the investment of temporarily idle funds which must above all things be kept liquid, are coming gradually to be recognized. The old prejudices, bred of ignorance or if you will of unfamiliarity with "acceptance" practice, are coming gradually to be broken down.

There is nothing in New York as yet, as has been said, to correspond with the phalanx of purely discount houses which for a century have served to attract to the London discount market the free banking capital of the world. Larger and larger each year, however, grows the number of our banks of deposit who not only themselves make a practice of "accepting" bills but who deal regularly in the acceptances of other banks and who encourage their inland correspondents to invest in this form of paper. Inevitably, as this has gone on, there has come into existence the entire machinery of distribution which can always be counted upon to develop wherever anything is being actively bought and sold. Alongside of the banks there have grown up a number of incorporated "discount companies"; alongside of these a number of private firms (largely the old "commercial paper" houses) which are specializing mainly in bills; and, cementing together the whole, the inevitable middleman, the bill broker, the man through whom a large proportion of the selling and buying is actually done.

The Discount Market and the Exchanges

A full discussion of the discount market and of the influences to which it is subject is, of course, no part of a work on foreign exchange. What we are mainly interested in, after all, is the effect which the existence of such a market has on the exchanges. Before the war we had no discount market. Now we have. What is the difference between the old condition and the new as it affects our financial relationship with the outside world?

Mainly, of course, greatly to increase the volume

of foreign exchange business actually done. Just as
this is written, for example, there is in progress a great
buying movement of American bank acceptances for
foreign account. Into London there has been pour-
ing a stream of outside banking capital so great as
completely to absorb the supply of sterling bills there
available at an attractive rate. Unable to find profit-
able employment in London, a substantial part of this
temporarily idle foreign banking capital is finding its
way into the bill market in New York. All of which
means, of course, that dollar exchange with which to
make the necessary remittances to this side must be
found. Such a condition, increasing as it does the
volume of exchange transactions, never obtained in
the olden days. European banks then as now kept
funds on deposit here and did at times make time loans
to this market. Employment of temporarily idle foreign banking capital in the American market was,
however, an unknown thing. There were, as a matter
of fact, no bank acceptances in existence at that time
into which such money could go.

Another important effect on exchange of the creation of the discount market has been to create a supply
of and a demand for American dollar drafts at points
all over the world where the dollar was simply not
previously known. How great a task it was and how
long it took to get foreign shippers to draw in dollars
on New York instead of in pounds on London we have
already seen. Be that as it may, however, the fact remains that to a great extent the change finally *was*
made. Where London was then, as New York is now,
used to "clear" these shipments of merchandise to

the United States, it is perfectly true, ultimate payment for the goods had eventually to be made by the country of importation. The *total amount* of drawings on New York has not of course been increased or decreased by the change in the method of financing but the character of the bills drawn has undergone complete alteration. Where under the old conditions final payment for the goods used to be made by having London draw sight drafts on New York (or by having New York send sterling drafts to London, which amounts to the same thing) payment for the goods is to-day being made by having the seller draw long drafts in dollars directly on the American buyer or on the American buyer's bank.

The above are, necessarily, more or less technical considerations and must not be allowed to obscure the real point which is this: Establishment of the discount market here has brought us into much closer touch with the money markets of the world than we were ever in before. The point of contact is the foreign exchange market. As Europe's interest in our discount market is increased, the volume of our foreign exchange business is increased.

Practical Foreign Exchange Operations

With the above outline of the foreign exchange and discount markets before us, we can proceed to consideration of the main uses to which all this mechanism is put. These dealers, these banks with their elaborate foreign exchange facilities—what do they really do? What are the actual sources of profit which have led to the wholesale establishment of foreign exchange departments by the banks during the past ten or fifteen years?

Briefly, the operations of the foreign exchange bankers in New York divide themselves into two classes. First, there are the operations where the banker functions as an intermediary, that is to say, for instance, where he buys bills from a customer who has bills to sell, and supplies bills (his own) to the customer who has remittances to make. Secondly, there are the operations not conducted in the normal course of business with customers, but where the banker is operating in the market strictly on his own account—where, for example, he sees a chance to make a profit buying a foreign currency in one market and selling it out in another. Overlapping, necessarily, to a certain extent, these functions of the foreign exchange banker constitute two very distinct forms of activity, which it will be well separately to consider.

While in his capacity as an intermediary the foreign exchange banker engages in a variety of operations a full description of which would be far outside the range of a work of this kind, the broad principle on which he operates to bring buyer and seller together is well within the scope of our discussion. That result, as we have seen in a previous chapter, is accomplished by the banker acting not as an agent for either buyer or seller but as principal who buys from one and sells to the other. Not, it may be well again to repeat, the same bills. From the customer who has exchange to sell he may buy a 90-day sight draft drawn, with bill of lading attached, against a shipment of cotton

from Galveston to Liverpool. To the customer who
wants a bill of exchange he may sell a sight draft
drawn by himself upon his correspondent bank in
London. Yet the net result of the operation is to
bring buyer and seller together just as much as though
the identical bill had been turned over from one to
the other. What really happens is that through the
medium of his deposit account in London and the use
of the discount market there, the American banker is
able to convert any and all kinds of bills of exchange
offered to him into any and all kinds of bills of exchange required by those who have remittances to
make.

Sales "Against" Purchases

What form does the actual operation take and how
does the banker realize his profit? Let us take, for
example, the simple case where against the purchase
of a commercial bill payable on demand the banker
sells his own demand bill: A customer, we will say,
brings into the bank for sale a draft for £2000 which
he has drawn on a firm in London to whom he has sold
some electrical equipment. The banker knows both
parties to the draft, the drawer and drawee, to be
reliable; the shipment to be a bona fide one; the draft,
in other words, one that will promptly be paid on
presentation. Whether or not he buys it, then, becomes a matter of price. For his own sight draft on
his London correspondent he knows he can realize
at the moment a rate, say, of $3.80. If then he can
buy this commercial bill at, say, $3.78 per pound he
can make a profit of $40 on the transaction. There is,

of course, no tying up of funds, no loss of interest. The money he uses to buy the commercial draft he realizes from the sale of his own bill. Nor, on the other side, is there any overdraft. The two bills, the one the banker has bought and the one the banker has sold, go forward on the same steamer. A week later, on the same day, his account in London is credited with £2000 and debited with £2000. In both London and New York his position is the same except for the $40 profit he has made.

How is it that at a time when the banker can sell his own sight draft at $3.80 he can get anyone to sell him a bill at $3.78? Simply because, in the very nature of things, a banker's bill drawn on a banker is bound to command a better price than a merchant's bill drawn on a merchant. Slight as it may be in the case of a well-known drawer and drawee, there is, nevertheless, an element of credit involved in the purchase of any commercial bill. Which element of credit, of course, is exactly what fixes the differential between the price of "bankers'" and "commercial." Where the maker of the commercial bill is known to be a very strong firm, the price he can realize for his bill will be only a little less than the current rate for bankers' drafts. Where he is not so well known, the differential widens. The stronger the commercial bill, in other words, the less profit there is in buying it. The amount of the banker's profit, to state it another way, is entirely according to the degree of risk he is willing to assume. Two cents per pound profit would, of course, be out of the question in the case of a really first class commercial name. Not, however, at all out of the question in the case of a name which the buying banker might know to be perfectly good and yet which might not be generally recognized in the bill market.

Where a long draft is drawn and sold by a banker against the purchase of a long commercial draft, the element of credit enters to an even greater degree. The banker in that case is obligating himself to make a payment out of his foreign balance against funds which will not be actually collected for sixty or ninety days. Obviously, a credit risk spread over such a period is an entirely different proposition from a credit risk limited to a week or ten days and with the banker in possession, at that, of the bill of lading, up to the very moment the draft is presented for payment. The strongest commercial houses only, it is plain, can find a buyer for such a type of bill and then only at a very considerable concession in price. However prime the names involved, the difference in price between a commercial long bill and a banker's long bill is at all times very considerably greater than the difference in price between a commercial sight bill and a banker's sight bill.

Time Bill Operations

To attempt to enumerate, let alone describe, all the various activities of the foreign exchange banker in his capacity as an "intermediary," would, as has been pointed out, carry us far beyond the purview of a work of this kind which, after all, is in no sense intended to be a manual of foreign exchange practice. One main activity of the banker, however, is of such great importance in its influence on the markets as to require that it be very definitely understood. Most inter-country purchases and sales of merchandise, we have seen, are financed by drafts of one sort or another drawn at 60 or 90 days' sight. Most requirements, on the other hand, for remittances with which to settle various debts due by the people of one country to the people of another country, are for bankers' drafts drawn payable "on demand" or for "cables." How does the banker in his capacity as intermediary oper-ate to make possible the immediate disposal for cash of these long-time commercial bills, and how does he place himself in a position to furnish his own sight drafts and cables to those in need of them?

At the risk of seeming to repeat ourselves, it is again to be pointed out that what is perhaps the most basic of all foreign exchange operations is the pur-chase by the banker of commercial long bills and the sale of his own sight drafts against such purchases. Assuming that the commercial bills are drawn upon a point where there exists an active money market in which they can be discounted, such bills, to the banker, are really in effect just so much sight ex-change which can and will be placed to the credit of his deposit account abroad immediately upon their arrival. A banker in New York, we will say for il-lustration, buys from an exporter a 90-day sterling draft drawn on a cotton spinner in Liverpool. Sent forward by the first available steamer, the draft is at once presented to the drawee. Upon its being "ac-cepted" it is immediately offered in the market for discount at whatever happens to be the prevailing rate (or at a rate previously arranged by cable), the proceeds being then credited forthwith to the American banker's deposit account. If the draft was originally, say, for £1000, the amount credited will, of course, be less than £1000 by the amount of the discount. That, however, in no way alters the fact that by the purchase and remittance of the 90-day cotton bill for £1000 the American banker has succeeded in getting his deposit account credited with practically £1000; and that on that increase in his balance he is free to draw his own sight draft.

The entire point to the operation of course, so far as the banker is concerned, is to be able to realize more dollars in New York from the sale of his newly created balance than it cost him to put the balance over there. The £1000 90-day cotton draft cost him in the first place, let us assume, $3750. After say 3% for 93 days (3 days of grace) and bill stamps were deducted from the face of the bill in the process of discounting, a net amount of perhaps £990 was placed to the credit of his account. If now he can sell his own sight draft for £990, for over $3750, the excess will constitute his profit.

Needless to say, the banker buying a long commercial bill from an exporter does not wait for the bill actually to be discounted and the proceeds to be placed to the credit of his account before drawing his own bill. The two operations, as a matter of fact are simultaneous, the price which the banker can get for his own draft being the determining factor in the price he is willing to pay for the commercial bill. If the discount rate in London is high, if in other words a considerable amount is going to be taken off the face of the commercial bill in the process of "discounting," then the price which the banker is going to be willing to pay for the bill will be relatively low. The higher the prevailing discount rate, to put it another way, the greater will be the spread between the price of long bills and of bills payable on demand.

All the above is written with full appreciation of the fact that at the present time, owing to the disturbed condition of credit both here and abroad, the bill drawn at 60 and 90-days' sight is playing a part in the foreign exchange market of far less importance than usual. That, however, one can hardly help but feel, is a temporary condition and one that will be superseded in due course by the use of long bills on a scale fully up to anything that has ever been seen in the past. The two, three and even four months' sight bill constitutes after all, the means by which the inter-country exchange of merchandise has been financed for the past several generations. Unless, then, we are to assume the advent of an entirely different order of things, it is logical to believe that as credit conditions again become normal, the long bill will be restored to its previous position of importance in international trade.

Commercial Credits

One other form of activity on the part of the foreign exchange banker in his rôle as intermediary remains to be mentioned, the granting of commercial credits. Infinite, however, as they are in variety, so

that a volume might be easily written about them without exhausting the subject, commercial credits all
work on the identical principle of the issuing banker's
being willing to step in and make temporary payment
for the merchandise. Whatever the character of the
transaction, whatever the form taken by the credit, the
net principle is always the same: Get your payment
from me, says the banker to the seller of the merchandise. The party over here to whom you are selling has
arranged to have you get your money from me instead
of from him. Draw your drafts on me according to
the terms of this commercial letter of credit I am issuing and they will be duly honored. Instead of paying
you your customer is paying me.

Out of these commercial credit operations originate
bills of exchange of every conceivable kind and form.
The deal made between the buyer and the seller of the
merchandise as to how payment is to be made—that,
of course, is what actually determines the nature of
the "credit." A shipper of bristles or wool from China
may demand that he be allowed to draw at ninety
days' sight in sterling on London or, on the other hand,
he may be willing to sell his bristles or wool only on
condition that he be allowed to draw a sight draft in
dollars on a New York bank. A Philadelphia firm
exporting machinery to Holland might draw sight
guilders on Rotterdam or, on the other hand, might
demand cash payment in dollars in New York; which
payment, of course, the Dutch importer would sooner
or later have to make in guilders at the current rate
of exchange. Of every kind and variety, as has been
said, are the bills originating from the extension of

these credits—long bills, short bills, bills in sterling, dollars, francs, guilders and every other form of currency.

Operations for Own Account

Turning now from consideration of the operations carried on as intermediaries to consideration of operations carried on by foreign exchange bankers for their own account, we find the most important of these, naturally, to be those based on estimated fluctuations in the rate of exchange. Reduced to their very simplest and most elemental form, such operations consist of the purchase of exchange when the operator figures that exchange is going up, or the sale of exchange when he figures that the rate is going down. Anything that has a fluctuating price and a big market lends itself to speculative operations, and foreign exchange is certainly no exception to the rule.

Where the operation is on the purchase side of bills payable at sight, the procedure is, of course, immediately to remit all bills purchased to the point at which they are payable, for credit of account. The normal balance in London of some American bank is, perhaps, £100,000. Believing that sterling exchange for example, is going to rise, the New York banker begins buying sterling bills in New York and, perhaps, in Paris or Amsterdam as well. These bills as they are bought are forwarded to London and credited to the New York banker's deposit account. Gradually his balance there is increased until it stands, perhaps at £300,000. What is really happening now is that the banker is speculating on the rate of exchange at which he will be able to sell out the £200,000 by which his balance now exceeds its normal amount. If his guess or as he prefers to call it his calculation on what the rate is going to do turns out to be correct, and sterling rises, say, from 3.70 to 3.80, the ten cent profit per pound is going to net him a gain of $20,000. If, on the other hand, the market goes ten cents against him and he decides he had better get out, he will have sustained a loss of that amount.

Foreign Exchange "Futures"

Another and extremely important way in which speculation for the rise and fall is carried on in exchange is through the purchase and sale of "futures." In foreign exchange as in wheat or stocks or anything else it is always possible for a responsible party to make a contract to deliver bills of exchange at a fixed price at some stated future time, or, on the other hand, so to receive bills. The foreign exchange "future," it is to be noted, is thus in no sense an "option." What it is, is a straight future contract to receive or deliver bills of exchange at a price.

How is it, it may well be asked, that somebody can always be found willing to enter on either side of such a contract, and at a price close to that currently prevailing? Simply because there are always people who know that one month, two months, three months from now, they will have bills of exchange to sell and who want to know exactly what they are going to get for them; and because there are other people who know that at a certain future time they will have to buy bills of exchange and who prefer thus to settle in advance the rate they are going to have to pay. Take the case of an American cotton shipper who, in August, sells cotton to a Manchester spinner for delivery in November. Three months after the sale is made, the shipper knows, he will have sterling bills to sell. How, unless he knows what he is going to get for those bills, can he figure where he is going to come out on the transaction? So what does he do? He makes a contract, or as the saying is he "sells a future," to deliver certain bills at a certain future time at a certain price. Or, to look at the other side of the picture, take the case of an American importer who has brought in raw silk from Japan for which he will have to make payment in sterling in London three months from now: How, unless he knows what he will have to pay for the necessary exchange, can he tell what the silk he has imported is actually going to cost him? So, to cut out the element of speculation and keep the transaction on a business basis, he "settles the rate" by buying a future. He contracts, in other words, to buy a certain amount of exchange at a certain future time at a certain price.

Here, then, just as we have people with "spot" bills to sell and others with bills to buy, we have a condition where there are people with futures to offer and others with futures to buy. Which, of course, again brings the foreign exchange banker into the picture, sometimes in his capacity as an intermediary, but more often as a principal operating for his own account. For him to speculate by buying bills without selling against them is all very well but ties up a lot of money after all, even for a banker. Here is a method of operating by which, without putting up any money at all, he can play either side of the market to any extent he sees fit. His judgment tells him, perhaps, that rates are going down: He can step in, in that case, and sell futures to those that want them. Or, if he figures that the market is going up, he can buy futures as they are offered. Without tying up a dollar, in other words, he can take a position either on the long side or short side of the market, as he sees fit.

Having entered into such a contract to buy or sell, it does not by any means follow that the banker must await the contract's actual termination to realize his profit or to take his loss. With the rate for regular demand exchange at 3.80, we will say, the banker has entered into a contract to receive and pay for £10,000 in three months, at 3.82½. A month goes by and sight sterling has risen, perhaps, to 3.88. That means that two months' futures (and what the banker originally bought, remember, has now become a two months' future) will be selling, perhaps at 3.86. Satisfied now with his profit of $350 and fearing that the market may not hold its advance, the banker may now very possibly decide either to turn his future over to somebody else or to sell his own future against it, which, of course, amounts to the same thing. Sixty days further along, then, he receives in £10,000, for which he pays out $38,250, and at the same time delivers out £10,000 of his own drafts, for which he receives $38,600.

How much or how little risk the operation in futures is to carry is something which he himself can determine. He can, as has been explained above, cut short his risk of profit or loss at any time during the life of the contract. Or he can, if he prefers not to sell his contract or his own futures against the contract, sell his own actual time bills, dated so as to coincide in maturity with the maturity of his contract to purchase. At no time, in other words, is he "locked in." If in a couple of weeks or a month the market does what he figured it might take it three months to do, he can take his profit and, except so far as the settlement of the technical details at the termination of the contract is concerned, he can take himself out of the transaction then and there. Or, on the other hand, if the market starts to go against him and he figures that he has made a mistake, he can sell his own future against what he has contracted to receive, take his loss, and get out. It is, incidentally, to be noted that it is among the operators in exchange who do retain an open mind and who, when they realize that they have made a mistake are willing to admit it and cut short their loss, that the greatest degree of success is usually to be found.

Public Speculation in "Futures"

Our current discussion, it is true, concerns itself with the operations in exchange of those who do it as a regular business, but it is of interest and importance to note in passing that it is through the purchase and sale of these "futures" that the speculatively minded outside public interested in exchange matters carries out its operations in exchange. An individual speculator, obviously, with no balance abroad and no recognized standing in the exchange market which would make possible "hedging" operations through the purchase and sale of long bills, is confined in his operations to the straight purchase and sale of futures. Those he can always buy and sell, often, if his credit is good enough, without putting up any money. Usually, however, the bank requires the deposit of margin—"protection," it is likely to be called—which margin, by the way, must be kept good if the market goes against him. The bank which has sold a future is quite likely at some stage in the operation, as we have seen, to have bought a future against its sale. That being the case, the bank will usually want to be very sure that the party which has contracted to take such-and-such bills off its hands three months further along, will not fall down on his agreement. To prevent the possibility of that there is just one sure way, and that is to require the deposit and keeping good of a margin sufficient to protect the seller of the future against any drop in the market which may take place. Then, if the rate does go down and the customer who has contracted to receive and pay for the bills cannot or will not make good, the bank will simply sell them to somebody else at whatever is at that time the current market and make good its loss out of the margin on hand.

Is then the buying and selling of foreign exchange futures a legitimate operation or is it just plain gambling? To that the answer must be that the legitimacy of dealings in exchange futures, like that of dealings in cotton futures or wheat futures or any other kind of futures, is purely and solely a matter of the purpose for which they are undertaken. The man who makes up his mind that the sterling rate or some other rate is going to be lower three months from now and who goes out and sells a future is engaging in a purely speculative operation. The man, on the other hand, who has contracted to ship goods abroad sixty or ninety days further along and who sells a future against the bills of exchange which he knows he will have on his hands for disposal at that time, is doing an entirely businesslike thing—is employing the only method possible, as a matter of fact, to keep the element of speculation out of the transaction. The whole thing, after all, is a matter of motive. Like submachine guns, cocaine and a number of other things which might be mentioned, exchange futures have their legitimate and their non-legitimate uses.

Arbitrage Operations

In our discussion of the main activities of the foreign exchange banker carried on in the market for his own account, we come finally to that class of operation made possible by the fact that, as previously explained, foreign exchange rates between two or more closely connected markets are continually tending to get out of line. Theoretically, as we have seen, rates between centers like London, Paris and New York maintain a state of "parity"—that is to say, the movement of any one rate so affects the others that all three are maintained in a state of equality. Practically, that is true, but only because of the buying and selling transactions in exchange in the various affected markets ("arbitrage" operations) which are undertaken by bankers whenever a momentary disparity in rates allows the chance to make a profit. All the time, then, rates are tending to get out of line and all the time, as a result of these "arbitraging" operations, they are being forced back to parity.

The very simplest form of arbitrage, as we saw early in this discussion, is between just two markets. In New York the cost of the pound sterling (cable) at some given time is, we will say, $3.80, which means, of course, that in London the cost of $3.80, in the form of a cable on New York, is one pound. Suppose, now, that in New York the appearance of a big selling order in pounds causes the rate suddenly to fall to 3.79½. Information as to what is happening will quickly enough find its way to London; but, in the meantime, and before the market in London has time to readjust itself, the alert New York arbitrageur may have his chance. Here in New York he can buy pounds, deliverable in London, at 3.79½ per pound. In London he can use those pounds to buy dollars, deliverable in New York, at $3.80 for each pound. For each $3.79½ he expends, then, he gets back $3.80, a profit sufficiently tempting to make him carry on the arbitrage on as large a scale and for as long as he possibly can. Eventually, of course, his own buying of sterling in New York and of dollars in London, and the buying of other bankers similarly engaged, will close up the momentary spread and put the two rates back to parity, where no further arbitrage is possible.

Where three rates instead of two are concerned, the arbitrage naturally becomes slightly more complicated. The principle, however, remains the same and should present no difficulties of comprehension.

For purposes of illustration, the rate for sterling cables in New York happens some day to be declining at
the same time that the rate for franc cables in New
York is advancing. What now about the rate for
francs in London? If for the moment that rate fails
correspondingly to advance, a "triangular" arbitrage
may become possible. In New York a sterling cable
for £10,000 on London can be bought, we will say, at
$3.75 per pound (cost $37,500). In London, where
the price of francs is, perhaps, 95.19 francs per pound,
the £10,000 can be used to buy a cable for fc. 951,900
on Paris. If now the cable rate for francs in New York
is 3.95 cents per franc, those 951,900 francs can be
sold out for $37,600.05. The original cost of the £10,-
000 having been $37,500, the arbitrageur is gainer on
the operation by $100.05.

If such a profit seems to the man accustomed to deal
in commodities or securities to be small, it must be
remembered that what we are talking about here is a
banking operation, practically without risk, and conducted invariably on a very large scale. Furthermore,
that while the amounts involved are large, the buying
and selling operations are simultaneously conducted.
The arbitrageur, in other words, is never out of the
use of his money. The funds he expends for the purchase of the sterling cable on London, he gets back at
once through the sale of the franc cable on Paris. On
his original capital he can, if he gets the chance, go
on arbitraging all day.

The operations of the exchange banker as intermediary and for his own account described above are

necessarily of the most elementary character and chosen mainly because of the principles they illustrate. To attempt a detailed description of the multifarious activities which daily occur in the foreign exchange department of any large bank would be to attempt to prepare a manual of foreign exchange practice. That task, interesting as it might be, is one which the author prefers to leave to someone with the urge to show the foreign exchange fraternity how better and more profitably to conduct their own business.

CHAPTER VII

INTER–GOVERNMENT DEBTS
AND CLAIMS

In our survey of the foreign exchanges it has seemed well thus far to confine ourselves to discussion of the debits and credits between countries arising from the operations of private parties, that is to say, of individuals, mercantile corporations and banks. We come now to what in the past few years has developed into a matter of transcendent importance, the financial relationship between governments. At the end of the War, by the signing of the Treaty of Versailles, we saw come into existence claims by various governments upon one another running into the tens of billions. Preceding and following the stroke of the pen which made or at any rate sought to make binding these reparations claims, we saw the creation of equally large claims by governments which during the world conflict and immediately thereafter had loaned great sums to other governments. Finally during the ten years following the end of the War there was witnessed the spectacle of governments, largely though not entirely by means of great bond issues, borrowing not from the governments of other countries but from individuals and institutions located in other countries.

For a clear understanding of to-day's exchange markets and the influences which to-day bear upon them, appreciation of the above circumstances will be found of the utmost importance. First the war-time munitions loans by the United States to England and France and the re-loaning, in effect, of those funds by England and France to their various allies. Then the fixing of reparations. Then the further "reconstruction loans" made by the U. S. A. after the end of the War and, following that, the flotation of huge foreign government bond issues in the American market. As a last step, in the battle to maintain exchange rates, the great "credits" established with our banks by the Bank of England and by the British Treasury. That, roughly, is the sequence.

Establishment of Credits

To go back to the beginning, the first step of course represents the financing of our allies during the period prior to our active military participation. England and France, and to an important though naturally a lesser degree our other allies, were under the necessity of buying huge supplies of munitions in this country. There was only one way in which these purchases could possibly be paid for and that was out of funds advanced by the American government. At the request then of Britain and France and the others, "credits" for very large amounts were established and out of these "credits" payment was made to the American manufacturers and others from whom the buying was being done. At no time, it is to be noted, did the money so used leave the country; though later, as a matter of fact, when dollars were being advanced to

Britain to enable her to maintain her exchange rate, not all the money was necessarily expended here. When, therefore, the statement is made, as in the preceding paragraph, that part of the funds advanced to its allies by the American government during the War was re-loaned by them, the qualification should be made that that is "in effect" what took place. If it was not actually the money advanced by us which was so re-loaned, such loans were nevertheless solely and only possible by reason of the credits established here —in other words, because England and France were not being required to send over money to pay for the goods which they were buying in this country. Had they been so required, the credits which they would have been able to extend would have been moderate indeed.

There was not at the time these first loans to Britain and France were made, it is to be noted in passing, any very definite understanding as to the form which repayment should take. Provision, it is true, was made that the hastily given notes of the British and other Treasuries should later be funded into regular interest-bearing bonds; but as to how and when the bonds should be paid, that question was left open. The exigency of the situation required that it should be so. England and the others had to have the goods —the winning of the War, in which we ourselves were by now involved, depended upon it—and there was no time for haggling about the question of repayment. Time for that, the feeling was, when the War is over and we are all again in a position to check up on the resources at our command.

Purpose of Credits

Following the loans for the simple purpose of payment for supplies came the loans made for the purpose of supporting the rate of exchange. Not all of England and France's buying in this country, of course, was being done with money advanced by the American government. To keep the pound and the franc up in relation to the dollar, therefore, became a matter of the very greatest importance. Knowingly then and willingly we advanced very large sums to be used for this purpose. Again and again credits in favor of the British Government were established in American banks, so that, when buyers of American goods in London started to buy the dollar exchange needed to pay for them, dollar drafts would be available and at not too great an advance in price. Serious indeed would have been the plight of the English buyers of American goods had their pounds sterling, instead of buying $4.86 worth of American goods as usual, fallen to a point where they would buy only, say, $3.86 worth. The time, be it remembered, was not one of cold commercial calculation, but of common cause. To ourselves as well as to them it was of the very greatest importance that these foreign buyers should be able to keep on getting the needed goods here. If in order to make that possible the exchange rate has got to be supported, the feeling was, we had better let them have the money with which to do the necessary supporting.

In order to buy munitions, then, in order to support the rate of exchange, and, finally, when the War came to an end, in order to assist in the work of reconstruction and rehabilitation, these direct government loans to England, France, Italy, Belgium and the other nations were made. With the German mark even at that time around 12 cents and the French franc around 18 cents, it was naturally not dreamed that post-war international finance would take the frightful course it did. We have loaned these countries billions to carry on the War, we felt, and if now it turns out to be necessary to loan them additional money to finish up the job and get them back on their feet, we had better go ahead and do it. They, after all, during their reconstruction period, are going to be tremendous buyers of our goods. And—the sooner they are back on their feet the better it will be for us, as for them.

As to the wisdom or unwisdom of the policy followed no opinion is here offered. Controversy plays no part in a discussion of this kind. What we are interested in now is not whether it was wise or foolish for us to advance all this money but rather as to what conditions affecting the foreign exchange markets were created by the fact that the advances were actually made. For the purchase of munitions, for the supporting of the exchange and finally for rehabilitation, a sum approximating $10,500,000,000 was loaned by the government of the United States directly to the governments of these various nations. And, of course, thereby there was created a state of affairs affecting the indebtedness between ourselves and these other countries most profoundly to affect the foreign exchanges for years to come.

Further Borrowings

Before proceeding to discussion of those conditions, however, we want to be very sure that we have the entire picture clearly in mind. There is, of course, a good deal more to it than the inter-government loans made during and just subsequent to the War. Almost as soon as the making of these direct advances came to an end, borrowing in this country by foreign governments was resumed on a tremendous scale, this time through the issue and sale of foreign government bonds in the American security markets. Previous borrowings above referred to had been between governments, with the public hardly aware of what was going on. What began now was a movement whereby these foreign governments and their subdivisions began, through the issue of interest-bearing bonds, to borrow directly from the American private investor.

During the decade following the end of the War, foreign borrowings in the American market amounted to $4,500,000,000. Beginning with issues by the stronger European governments and bearing high rates of interest, the movement gradually acquired momentum until, within a comparatively short space of time, bonds were being sold here in large amount not only by governments, but by foreign states, municipalities and finally by private corporations. Once awakened, there seemed to be no limit to the American investor's appetite for the foreign high-interest-bearing bond. Anything and everything offered was eagerly taken, anything from the bonds of the old and admittedly strong governments to those of gov-

ernments created as a result of the Treaty—where it
was literally necessary, in many cases, for the sales-
man to tell the buyer in what part of Europe the
country whose obligations he was buying was actually
located.

It is worth while perhaps to pause for a moment to
note the reason for the tremendous vogue acquired by
these foreign bonds almost from the moment they began to be issued. First and foremost, no doubt, was
the high return offered on the investment, coupons
calling for seven, seven-and-a-half and even eight percent. Secondly, there was the so prevalent feeling that,
a war of such proportions having just ended and the
probabilities being that there would not be another
war for a very long time, the obligation of practically
any government was bound to be all right at least for
a term of years. Thirdly, there was the fact that the
American investor had had absolutely no experience
with foreign bonds, government or otherwise, and had
no yardstick whatever with which to measure their
value. Generally speaking he could of course tell
that the bonds of old established and compactly constituted governments like Holland and Switzerland
were a safer proposition than those of the newly established governments made up of all sorts of racial
diversities, but it was just about there that his knowledge of the subject came to an end. Almost never, especially when the issues began to come one after the
other and to go to a premium almost as soon as offered,
did he stop to inquire as to the purposes for which the
money was to be used or as to the national resources
from which repayment was to be provided. Especially

by the South American governments and subdivisions, loan after loan was made in this country where it should have been perfectly plain not only to the issuing bankers but to any inquiring investor that there was no reasonable probability of sinking fund and interest payments being kept up for any length of time.

Again, however, it becomes necessary to veer away from the controversial aspect of the matter. The point, after all, is not whether the foreign borrowers were justified in taking advantage of the insatiable demand for foreign bonds which existed at that time but, rather, that the bonds *were* sold and that the obligations to pay were entered into. In other words, that within the comparatively short space of ten years there was added to the 10½ billions of dollars owed directly to the U. S. Government a further amount of 4½ billions of dollars owed to private investors and institutions.

Credits to Support Exchange

To complete the picture there must be mentioned the $650,000,000 borrowed by the Bank of England and the British Government late in the summer of 1931, $325,000,000 of it here and $325,000,000 in France, in its heroic effort to sustain the exchange rate and keep from going off the gold basis. All through the early summer of '31, it will be recalled, and this at a time when Britain's foreign loans were "frozen" in Germany and elsewhere, London was being called upon to return the French and other short term capital deposited there. Withdrawals between the first of July and the middle of September (when the gold standard was finally abandoned) amounted to £200,000,000, during which time the rate for sterling was naturally subjected to very great pressure. Large amounts of gold were shipped from England, the gold reserve of the Bank falling during that two months' period from £166,000,000 to £135,000,000, but in spite of everything the exchange rate on London continued to decline. If the situation was to be saved and the gold standard maintained, it became evident, the fall in the exchange must be arrested. To accomplish that end or rather to try to accomplish it, the British Treasury and the Bank obtained credits from the Federal Reserve Bank and the Bank of France as well as from separate syndicates of French and American banking houses, aggregating the immense sum of $650,000,000. With these funds at its command the British Government waged a determined struggle to protect the pound, buying at times all the sterling bills offered on the foreign markets and at other times furnishing to the London banks the franc and other foreign currency drafts which the frantic demands of their overseas depositors were requiring them to provide. Of no avail, however, were these efforts, the amount of short term foreign capital in London subject to withdrawal being so great and the demands of its owners for its return being so urgent that eventually the Bank of England's buying power was overwhelmed and the exchange rate started swiftly downward. Then, of course, there was nothing left to do but to suspend gold payments, any

other course meaning the rapid depletion of the
Bank's remaining gold reserve.

Repayment of practically the entire amount of
$650,000,000 thus borrowed in America and France
has, as this is written a little less than a year later,
been already accomplished. So far as its influence
on the exchange market is concerned, therefore, the
incident is closed. To have omitted it from any sum-
up of post-war intergovernmental borrowing operations would, however, to have been to leave the picture incomplete.

Central Bank Deposits

In our discussion of these special post-war inter-
government debit and credit situations, we come now
to the condition created by the maintenance, by various governments, of large deposits in countries outside their own. As a concomitant of close financial
relationships between countries, deposit accounts, as
we have seen, have always been maintained by the
bankers of one country with the bankers of another.
The maintenance of such balances by governments,
particularly by great governments, is, however, a development only of the past decade, and has brought
about a condition of things in the exchange markets
with which they never hitherto have had to deal.

The most conspicuous case in point, of course, is
the great fund maintained on deposit by the French
government with the banks in New York. Accumulated in large part some time prior to the resumption
by France of the gold standard in June of 1928, these
balances grew in size until by the middle of 1931 they

are believed to have approximated the sum of three quarters of a billion dollars. A similar deposit account, though of considerably smaller size was maintained by the French government in London.

The original purpose of the establishment of these large deposit accounts was, of course, the protection of the rate of exchange. Prior to 1928, when France was off the gold standard, the stability of the franc while important to French trade and industry was in no sense vital. With the resumption of specie payments and of an unrestricted gold market in Paris, that was of course no longer the case and it became imperative that the franc be sustained in its relation to the dollar. In one way and in one way only, through the maintenance of large dollar balances with the New York banks, could that result be definitely assured. As long as the French government was in a position to tell its agents in New York to absorb all offerings of bills drawn on Paris, the rate of exchange could not materially decline.

The same thing was done in London as in New York and in the same careful and painstaking manner. Gradually, for a period of fully a year and perhaps more, before the French gold market was thrown open, sterling balances were being accumulated in the London banks just as dollars were being accumulated here. Then, finally, when the French fiscal authorities felt their position sufficiently strong, when they were at last entirely convinced of their ability to take care of whatever selling of franc exchange might develop, the doors of the Paris gold market were thrown open to the world. Here we stand, said the French, ready to exchange gold for francs: If you in America or you in England can buy francs cheap enough to make it pay you to send them over here and exchange them for gold, go ahead and do it.

What happened then, as is well known, and as is proved by the way in which the French government's balances in New York steadily *increased*, was that instead of the expected selling movement in francs a steady buying movement actually set in. France is back on the gold basis, the feeling seemed to be, and, heeled with these big dollar balances here in New York, she is in a position there to stay. With the Bank of France able and willing, through its American agents, to absorb all offerings of drafts on Paris, where then is the chance of any sizable decline in the franc? The thing to do under the circumstances is, evidently, not to sell francs but rather to buy them. Which is exactly what then did happen—with the result that from then on (June 1928) there was never a month in that year or the next when the average rate for francs in New York went below .0391 cents per franc (par .039179).

Exactly the same thing took place in London. Skeptical at first, the British market, which itself had at the time been back on a gold basis for only a little over three years, soon enough became convinced that the Bank of France was not only determined but well able to maintain the position of the franc as against the pound and, so, began buying instead of selling the French currency. Just as had taken place in New York, the deposits of the Bank of France, instead of being heavily drawn upon, began actually to increase.

To the point under discussion, the importance of the above lies in the fact that within a couple of years after France's resumption of the gold standard, the deposits of the Bank of France in the private banks both of New York and London had attained proportions very much greater, in all probability, than it had ever been planned originally that they should be allowed to attain. Why these balances were ever allowed to accumulate as they were will ever remain a matter open to argument. Possibly the more favorable interest rates prevalent in London and particularly in New York had a good deal to do with it. Possibly the real explanation lies in the fact that, having gone back on the gold standard, the French government was determined to go the limit in making impregnable its newly assumed position. Be that as it may. The fact remains that by the beginning of 1931 the French government had on deposit in New York a sum estimated at not far from three quarters of a billion dollars and that in London a further very large sum, though possibly not as great as that in New York, lay deposited to its credit, *withdrawable on demand*.

French Deposits in London

We must not, in this treatise on the nature and theory of the foreign exchanges allow ourselves to be led into too detailed a description of contemporary events. What happened, however, after the deposit accounts of the Bank of France in New York and London reached the proportions they did, so perfectly illustrates the principle at issue, that its clearest possible exposition lies probably in a simple narration of the events themselves.

Briefly, London, during the early part of 1931, had made large short-term loans in the German and other Continental markets. Money rates in England, to a large extent as a result of the French balances there, had become so low that the English banks were more or less forced to go outside the country in order to find employment for their idle funds. The situation in Germany, while not in the best of shape, had at that time given no indication of the distressing conditions to come. We ourselves, it will be recalled, were at that time employing large amounts of short-term capital in the German market, and no hesitation was felt by our banks in lending the German government a sum amounting to as much as $125,000,000. If it seems strange now that at the time the storm broke in Berlin the English bankers should have been caught with very large deposits there, it must be realized that their mistake in judgment was no different from our own. To the experienced bankers both of London and New York, the Berlin market, during the early months of 1931, seemed a safe and profitable place in which to be lending money.

Even when it developed that that was anything but the case, London might well have been able to see the situation through without being knocked off the gold basis had the French adopted a less insistent attitude with regard to the return to them of their London deposits. In London's long experience as the world's banker there had been other occasions when her short-term loans in other markets had become temporarily frozen; but never a time when, under such circumstances, her own creditors were clamoring insistently for the return of their funds. That, of course, was what made London's position so bad—not only that her own money was tied up in Germany but that the French banks began demanding immediate repayment of their London deposits and began taking them in the form of gold.

Withdrawal of Deposits

We have here, then, the perfect illustration of the control exerted over one market by another market to which the first is indebted on a large scale. London for a hundred years had been accustomed to receiving and handling the deposits of outsiders and to returning those deposits, when wanted, on short notice. The single deposit of some hundreds of millions by the Bank of France and the deposits of the private French banks was, however, something entirely different from anything ever seen before. Without in the least realizing it at the time, the London banks when they accepted those deposits and let them grow to the size they did, were putting themselves completely within the French market's power. That conditions could develop which would ever result in the deposits being suddenly and ruthlessly withdrawn they never dreamed. Yet just that is exactly what happened, with the result that gold poured out at such a rate as to imperil the reserves of the Bank and to make it necessary for the British government to admit its inability to pay its notes in gold and, finally, to abandon the gold standard altogether.

For several months after that the dollar deposits in New York of the French government, larger by far than the deposits in London had ever been, lay virtually untouched. Then for reasons a discussion of which at this time would only lead us into a highly controversial field, the French government gave notice of its intention to repatriate these funds. The purpose of insuring the stability of the franc, it was announced, had been accomplished; a change in policy had been determined on by which the gold reserve of the Bank of France would no longer to any extent be allowed to remain overseas but would be kept within the vaults of the Bank itself.

The methods of withdrawal differed materially in the case of the funds on deposit in New York from those which had been employed in the case of the deposits in London. Frightened at the possibility that London might go off the gold standard before her deposits were all returned, France had, six months previously, adopted methods of getting her funds out of London which, in all probability, contributed in no small degree to bringing about that very condition which she feared. This time the same mistake would not again be made. The position in the United States, it was recognized, was very much stronger than it had been in London six months before; but, even so, there was danger in precipitate action. Sudden withdrawal of well over half a billion dollars of deposits, entailing, as it inevitably would, exports of gold amounting to at least a couple of hundred millions, would be a severe shock to any market, regardless of how well fortified that market might be. Better this time, the French bankers figured, to proceed with more care and to avoid doing anything which might result in prejudicing the purpose which it was sought to accomplish.

Instead, then, of beginning a wholesale drawing of drafts on its various deposit accounts and of forcing these drafts on to an unwilling market, the Bank of France quietly notified the banks in New York of its intention materially to reduce its American balances. Withdrawal of these funds, it was stated, would be spread out over a period of several months; and, in the meantime, at least such was the inference, nothing would be done in any way to disturb the exchange market. Undoubtedly, it was pointed out by the French authorities, the withdrawal from America of so large a sum, however carefully handled, would necessitate the export of gold in substantial amount; but, due notice having thus been given, that could easily enough be taken care of. The gold-carrying facilities of the fast steamers sailing within the next five or six weeks could, it was suggested, be arranged for in advance. As to the gold itself, that had better be "earmarked" at the Federal Reserve Bank, so that it would be generally understood what was going on, and so that no undue feeling of uneasiness would be allowed to develop over a series of gold shipments mysterious and unexplained.

"Earmarked" Gold

It will perhaps be worth our while here to pause for a moment and to note the meaning of this term "earmarked," which in the past few years has come to be so freely used in connection with foreign exchange. To earmark a thing is, of course, to label it and set it aside for some particular purpose, and that is precisely the meaning of the term as applied to the inter-country movement of gold. A foreign Central Bank, for example, having on deposit in another country a substantial amount of money which it intends a little further along to withdraw in the form of gold, or which it wants to use as an overseas gold reserve, will often instruct the bank in which the funds are on deposit to set aside with the government gold agency (in the U. S., the Federal Reserve Bank) a certain stipulated amount. The amount thus set aside, "earmarked," as the saying is, becomes thus virtually a deposit of gold with the Federal Reserve Bank, withdrawable at any time at the will of the owner. Where, before, the foreign Central Bank had a regular deposit with some private banking institution, it now has to its credit with the Federal Reserve a sum of gold which it can at any time order to be shipped. The owner may, after it is thus "earmarked," withdraw the gold at once. He may on the other hand, if it better suits his purpose, allow the gold to remain where it is for weeks or even months.

To all intents and purposes gold thus earmarked at the Federal Reserve Bank is the same as gold held in the vaults of the foreign Central Bank itself. It is simply a matter of location.

Gold thus earmarked, of course, passes out of the banking picture as completely as though it were actually put on a ship and sent out of the country. On the books of the foreign Central Bank's depository, it figures as a deposit withdrawn. On the books of the Federal Reserve, it figures as gold which has been bought, paid for and actually exported. Only in the statement of the foreign Central Bank does it show —there, of course, as gold actually held in vault.

What then, it may be asked, is the idea of ear-marking gold? Assuming, as in the case of a free gold market like New York it is to be assumed, that a deposit in any one of the great banks can at any moment be converted into gold, what has the foreign Central Bank to gain by thus taking in advance the steps preliminary to exportation? As a deposit in a private bank the funds draw interest, can be used for example for the purchase of instantly salable acceptances, etc. As earmarked gold at the Federal Reserve, the funds are sterile, earn no more than they would if they were afloat on a ship in the form of gold ingots. Why is it then that this practice of earmarking has grown to such an extent that there is to-day as this is written a sum in excess of three hundred million dollars earmarked for foreign account at the Federal Reserve?

The answer, undoubtedly, is to be found in the fact that it is a great convenience to the foreign Central Banks to be able to carry a part of their required gold reserves at a point where those reserves can, at short notice, be converted into supplies of foreign exchange. For earmarked gold can, of course, at any time at the will of the owner be "released from earmark." A time comes, we will say, when one of the Central Banks carrying earmarked gold at the Federal Reserve in New York, needs a supply of dollar exchange. Instead of having to go out into the market to buy the bills, perhaps at a high rate, the Bank is in a position to get the dollar exchange it needs simply by cabling the Federal Reserve. Release so-and-so-much of our gold under earmark, the instructions read, and credit the proceeds to such-and-such a bank. And so, without the expensive and in these days often difficult question of an exchange rate coming into the matter at all, the needed supply of dollar exchange is made instantly available. A sort of double-barrelled proposition—a convenient way of carrying reserves and at the same time being at all times assured of an adequate supply of foreign exchange—no wonder this practice of earmarking gold has grown to the extent it has.

"Available" Gold

From the foregoing and the figures given as to the size reached by foreign deposits in the New York market, it will be evident that we are dealing with an influence of the very first magnitude—an influence, by the way, whose importance seems to have been little understood during all that time when we were figuring that with "half the world's gold supply concentrated here" this market must necessarily be in an impregnable position. Half the world's gold supply *was*, it is true, concentrated here, but with a call upon it in the shape of a billion dollars of foreign bank deposits to which entirely too little consideration, unfortunately, was at that time given. The deposit account of a foreign bank, it must be remembered, is not, like a domestic deposit, something which may be shifted around but which when it is drawn down at one point reappears at another. A foreign deposit is not, like a domestic deposit, a call merely upon the reserve by which it is secured, but a call upon an amount of gold equal to the whole amount of the deposit.. The general estimate, then, of the amount of gold "available" in the country when the trouble began at the end of 1929 was really very far from being correct. From it there should have been deducted the full amount of the deposits of the foreign banks, private and government. We should never in all probability have viewed the situation with quite the complacency we did had we realized at the end of '29 that at least a billion dollars of our huge "available" gold supply could not with any justice be regarded as being available at all. The gold to be sure was there but, upon it, there were claims prior to our own. As long as everything was going along smoothly and the foreign deposits were allowed to remain where they were, we could use them—and how we did use them!—in the erection of our glorious credit pyramid. Demand for their return, however, soon enough opened our eyes to what was what. That we were able to come through as we did stands everlastingly to the credit of the American banking system. Though, at that, in order to put ourselves in a position where we *could* return to the foreigners their gold, it was necessary for us to amend the Federal Reserve Act so as to make it lawful, if necessary, to substitute government bonds for part of the gold held against our outstanding issues of Federal Reserve notes.

We learned at that time, as the British had learned six months previously, something we had not known before about the possible effects of inter-government bank deposits on the grand scale!

CHAPTER VIII

GOVERNMENT CONTROL OF EXCHANGE RATES

THE picture sketched in the previous chapter suggests very clearly that in the foreign exchange markets of today other and important influences bear upon rates in addition to those arising from the mere interchange of goods and securities and services and the other things which used to make rates go up and down. A copy of the Statistical Abstract, evidently, and the current figures on foreign trade, are no longer all that is necessary as a gauge of the exchange market's position. We shall need to take into account as well, it is plain, the intense interest which the fiscal authorities of the various governments have come to have in the foreign price of their respective currencies, and the many and varied methods they are now constantly employing to control the rate of exchange.

To insure a clear understanding of what is to follow about the way in which the various government financial agencies work to influence exchange rates, it will be well perhaps to make certain that we quite appreciate the purposes which motivate such action. First and foremost, no doubt, there must be placed the desire, through the maintenance of exchange rates where that is possible, to protect the integrity of gold reserves. Secondly, there is the desire, where maintenance of exchange rates has been found to be impossible and reserves have had to be protected by abandonment of the gold standard, to hold the rate of exchange, at whatever level it may have sought, on as even a keel as possible. Thirdly, where it has been possible neither to keep the rate at parity or even steady at a point somewhat below, there is the natural unwillingness on the part of any government to allow the rate of exchange to fall to so low a point as to endanger its commercial relations with the outside world.

Integrity of Gold Reserves

Let us consider first the incentive to hold the exchange at par or at a level slightly below. Failure to do that, as we have seen, assuming that a country is on the gold basis, means the throwing open of the door to its gold supply. Let the rate on any country fall below par by an amount even slightly in excess of the cost of shipping gold, and instantly gold will start flowing out. Then, unless the country in question is so well supplied with gold that it can afford to lose an amount which will in itself prove the necessary corrective, one of two things is bound to happen: First, either the government of the country on which the exchange has become depreciated will have to take the steps necessary to get the rate up again or admit its inability to continue doing business with the rest of the world on a gold basis. Secondly, it may choose, as so many countries in recent years have done, nominally to cling to the gold standard, while prohibiting exports of the precious metal; which, so far as its outside relationships are concerned, amounts to exactly the same thing as abandonment of the gold standard. Nobody of course is going to be willing to pay par or anything like par for a draft on a country out of which he knows in advance he will be unable to get his money after his draft has been cashed.

A further strong incentive to maintain the rate of exchange exists when a country is in the position of having to make substantial payments in other countries. A government, we will say, has borrowed heavily abroad through the issue of bonds and is under the necessity of making payments on account of interest, sinking funds and, perhaps, of maturities. If now its exchange is to depreciate in relation to the currency of the country in which the payments have to be made, by so much more is the difficulty of making those payments increased. Canada, for example, and her Provinces, during all the years when the Canadian dollar sold firmly on a par with the American dollar, borrowed hundreds of millions of dollars in the United States on the express stipulation that interest and principal should be payable in New York in United States funds. No one at the time thought that there was any danger of the Canadian dollar ever falling to a substantial discount. Yet that is exactly what did happen, the discount at the time this is written ranging around 10% and having at one time been close to twice as much. On the Canadian government and Provincial bonds not yet due and payable, the question of discount does not of course enter; but on the question of the interest on those bonds due and payable in New York every six months, it certainly does enter and to a most marked degree. Every dollar which the Canadian government and its subdivisions has to pay in New York funds is today costing them a dollar and ten cents in their own money to make. That is of course a heavy charge but, at that, nothing to what it was costing some of the lesser European and practically all the Latin-American countries for debt service on their American-held bonds at the time so many of them threw up their hands and declared themselves no longer able to pay. Of the very greatest importance, evidently, in such cases, is the maintenance of the rate of exchange where that is humanly possible.

Stable Rates and Foreign Trade

Finding it impossible to maintain its exchange rate at or close to par, a government has yet a very great incentive, after the rate has found its new level under the current conditions, to stabilize the rate at that level and to prevent too great fluctuations in either direction. In matters of foreign exchange, as of prices or wages or anything else, it is a truism that the business of a country can adapt itself to practically any given conditions provided those conditions remain fairly dependable and constant. What business cannot stand, particularly business done with a foreign country, is uncertainty as to the conditions under which the financing is to be done. Nothing exerts so restraining an influence on both exports and imports as an unstable and undependable rate of exchange.

That this is so will readily appear from a moment's

consideration of the extent to which the fixing of buying and selling prices in foreign trade are tied in with the rate of exchange. Take, for example, the case of an American importer bringing in wool from China. He may do his buying in American dollars or he may do it in Shanghai taels; but in either case the rate of exchange between Shanghai and New York is bound to be a governing factor in the making of the price. If the wool is bought in American dollars, the price quoted by the Chinese seller will of course be influenced by the rate at which he will have to convert the dollar proceeds of the sale into his own currency. If the wool is bought in taels the price which the American buyer will be willing to pay will similarly be influenced by the rate of exchange at which he will have to secure the taels with which to make payment. There is no getting away from it; where the buyer and the seller work in different currencies, the rate of exchange between the two kinds of money is bound to have a most important influence on any business done between them.

If then an exchange rate is in a highly unstable condition, with rates up one day and down the next, it is evident that commercial trading between those two points is rendered extremely difficult and at times even impossible. Theoretically the rate of exchange at the time the purchase or sale is negotiated is an ascertainable quantity and is used in determining the price. Practically, however, the matter is not so simple, the bargaining process involved in the purchase of the goods often covering several days and having perhaps to be consummated without regard to what was the rate of exchange at the time the negotiations were begun. The wool importer, to be more specific, may at the beginning have had a firm bid from an American mill at so-and-so-much per pound, which, with Shanghai exchange as then quoted, would have allowed him to bring it in at a satisfactory profit. In the event, however, that the purchase abroad takes a couple of days to make, and that, in the meantime, the rate of exchange goes away up, all the profit may be weaseled out of the trade and it may, indeed, be made entirely impossible.

On the part of the government and the banks of countries whose exchange rates are liable to sudden and violent fluctuations there is, thus, a very great incentive to hold the rate within limits to the greatest extent possible. Failure to do so means loss of trade. Continually balked through violent movements in exchange in their efforts to do business with a country suffering from a hopelessly unstable currency, merchants in other countries soon enough turn elsewhere to do their buying and selling.

Maintenance of Trade Relationships

The third purpose motivating a government to intervene in the natural course of exchange, is to support rates at times when they threaten to sink to levels so low as to make trading with other countries impossible. A comparatively low rate of exchange, as is explained further along, is an actual stimulus to export business, but beyond a certain point works the other way. No nation can keep on exporting on any considerable scale without importing substantially as well. If then the rate of exchange gets down to a point where a country's currency loses its buying power in the outside markets and imports of goods are made impossible, export business suffers as well.

The correction of such a situation, the support of such a rate of exchange, is, as we shall see in our examination of the ways in which governments operate to control the rate of exchange, a difficult matter indeed. We are here dealing with a condition, it is plain, the remedying of which calls for measures far more drastic than mere supporting purchases of exchange by the government or its fiscal agents. Constantly sinking rates are, after all, nothing but the visible evidence of conditions maladjusted; and it is those which must by government action be remedied before trade relations on a satisfactory basis can with the outside markets be resumed.

Control through Regulation of Merchandise Movement

There are very cogent reasons, it will appear from the above, for the government interference with the natural course of the exchange markets which is continually being seen. Just how that intervention is accomplished, just what means a government has at its disposal for the influencing of exchange rates—that, logically, is the next thing to be considered.

Since it is the in-and-out movement of merchandise which primarily affects any exchange rate, is it not logical that it should be through the control of exports and imports that government control of exchange rates is most effectively accomplished? Such is indeed the case. There are, as we shall see as we progress, at least three or four ways in which a government can operate to control the rate of exchange of its money with that of other countries, but none anywhere near as effective as its ability to regulate the in-and-out movement of merchandise. We strike there directly at the root of the matter. Less true, of course, in the case of great nations where banking and security-trading relationships play so important a part, it is a fact nevertheless that in the case of a very great majority of countries it is primarily demand and supply of commercial bills which shape the course of the exchange markets. Influence that demand and supply, and you come pretty close to influencing the rate of exchange itself. Make it easy to export and hard to import merchandise, and the effect upon rates will make itself quickly enough felt.

Can a government, then, say to its citizens, So-and-so-much in the way of merchandise shall you be allowed to send out of the country and so-and-so-much shall you be allowed to bring in? It certainly can, with the qualification that imports are naturally much easier to control than are exports. Try as it may, a country may at times be unable to accomplish much in the way of making the outside world buy more of its products, that is to say, in the way of increasing its exports. About the control of imports, however, there is never any difficulty. That is a purely government function and, through proper legislation, easily exercised.

Tariffs and "Quotas"

For purposes of illustration let us take the case, say, of any of the Latin-American countries where because of continued imports of American merchandise at a time of exceedingly poor prices for the goods ordinarily exported, the rate of exchange on New York and London has fallen to a very low point. About increasing the money value of exports, it is plain, there is not very much that can be done: The coffee and wool and other things these countries produce and sell have gone away down in price, and while the government may do everything in its power to make it easy to export, the total value of what the country has to offer for sale remains far below normal. Imports, however, are an entirely different proposition and entirely within the government's control. So what does the government do? Start erecting tariff barriers, in all probability, with a view to making it harder to bring goods in. First, perhaps, a moderate tariff designed merely to hold the import movement of goods within bounds. Then, if results are not satisfactory, schedules designed to operate more effectively. Finally, if goods in too large quantity continue to come in over the tariff wall, a set of rates which, in connection with the already depreciated purchasing power of the country's currency, will result in shutting out foreign goods entirely.

Without at this time entering upon any discussion of tariff policies, it is plain that important disadvantages attach to the erection of tariffs so high as completely to shut out imports. Even assuming that we are talking about a country which can get along without foreign goods for its own consumption, it must be borne in mind that the world's exports are to a large extent made up of manufacturers of raw materials which have previously been imported. That is, of course, not true, for example, of the South American countries whose exports consist almost exclusively of agricultural and animal products, but it is true of the exports of most countries engaged in foreign trade on a substantial scale. England, to mention only one example, produces only a very small part of the raw materials which form the basis for the enormous volume of her exports of fabricated products. Every yard of the fabrics, for instance, produced by the Lancashire mills, has first to be imported in the form of raw cotton.

Tariffs, however, by no means provide the only means by which imports can be controlled. A further and most efficacious way in which that can be accomplished is through the imposition of what are known as import quotas. Such restrictions in different countries take on various forms but the idea is always the same: Such-and-so-much value only of such-and-such goods to be admitted into the country in a given length of time. When the total has been reached, the matter is ended; no more goods of that particular kind can be brought in until the beginning of the next quota period.

Quota arrangements, naturally, are a matter of placing the limitations where they will do the most good, where they will most directly influence the exchange rates which it is sought to influence. They are, too, to a large extent, the subject of bargaining between countries. You increase the amount of our wines which you are willing to admit, says Spain to Norway, and we will raise our quota on your fish. Then, of course, it becomes a matter of expediency. What will be the net effect, the Norwegians have to consider, of an increase in the supply of bills drawn against shipments of fish and of an increase in the demand for bills to pay for the additional imports of wine? According as the answer shapes up, the proposition is likely to be accepted or rejected.

Rationing the Supply of Exchange

An even more positive way of controlling imports and one which as this is written is being used all over the world, is the rationing of the supply of foreign exchange. All open market dealings in bills, in this case, are done away with, the Central Bank being designated as the only place where foreign exchange can be bought and sold. A merchant having made a shipment to a foreign country and having drawn a draft on the buyer in the buyer's currency, does not, as usual, offer the draft around and try to find the bank which will pay him the best price for it. There is only one place where he can sell it and that is the government Foreign Exchange Agency, and there is only one price he can get for it and that is the rate officially fixed. Similarly, the importer of goods in need of a foreign draft to pay for something he has bought abroad, does not shop around among the banks as formerly, but goes direct to the Exchange Agency.

There and there only, if he can buy it at all, can he buy the draft he needs.

As a matter of fact, in all of these countries where the supply of exchange is being rationed, little or no importing is being done without the purchase of the necessary exchange having been arranged for in advance. Before, indeed, a purchase abroad can be made, permission must be obtained from the Exchange Agency. If permission is granted, the importer knows he is safe in going ahead. He knows that when the time comes to pay he will be able to secure the necessary exchange and at what price.

What then determines the answer which the importer is going to receive on his application? Largely, it is plain, the supply of foreign exchange, present and prospective, in the hands of the Exchange Agency. If exports are running heavy and the Agency has on hand a plentiful supply of bills, favorable consideration is likely to be given the importer's application. If, on the other hand, the Agency's supply of exchange is low, or if perhaps exchange is being accumulated against an expected demand for bills to pay for imports of a necessitous character, the chances are that the importer's application will be turned down. Always remembering, of course, that the kind of goods he is proposing to bring in will have a good deal to do with it. Especially in the case of a country where the supply of exchange is short, it is plain, for example, that an application to import raw material that is going to be manufactured and reëxported will meet with consideration very different from that accorded an application to bring in some luxury that will be immediately consumed.

Stimulation of Exports

Through tariffs, through quotas and through rationing, the import of merchandise, it is evident, can easily enough be controlled. Stimulation of exports is, however, another and far more difficult proposition. There are certain things a government can do to make it easy to export but, after all, it is the prospective customer abroad who has the say as to whether he will or will not buy.

Financial assistance to exporters is of course a government's most effective way of stimulating shipments to foreign countries. Particularly in these days of disturbed foreign exchange conditions, financing constitutes one of the principal obstacles to inter-country trade. When, therefore, through government aid to exporters, terms of payment are made easy, considerable sales resistance is broken down.

It is easy, in other words, to buy from a party who, having a strong financial backer, is able to offer liberal terms. Also, in that case, the question of price comes in. With the government offering what in some instances amounts practically to a subsidy, manufacturers are able to produce and offer goods for overseas shipment at prices which, if they had to depend entirely upon their own resources, they would never be able to quote. From a domestic standpoint, perhaps, there are certain "outs" on having the government thus closely connected with a country's commercial business; but of the effectiveness of such a policy in stimulating exports there is no possible question.

This whole question of government control of exchange rates through limitation of imports and stimulation of exports ties in so closely with what we have next to consider, government purchases and sales of exchange for the purpose of influencing rates, that it has seemed worth while to give it considerable attention. Where a government seeks closely to control the in-and-out movement of merchandise, we have seen, handling of the resulting foreign exchange transactions becomes automatically a government function. That, however, may be regarded as more or less incidental and is, in reality, a very different thing from the direct manipulation of exchange rates by large-scale government buying and selling which is about to be described. For Persia, for example, to decree that no one can import goods without having first exported goods of an equal value is one thing; for Britain to announce the creation of a £150,000,000 fund for the purpose of controlling exchange rates is quite another.

Government Purchases of Exchange—"Pegging" during the War

We shall perhaps arrive most readily at a clear understanding of how governments operate through purchases and sales of bills to control the rate of exchange, if we take one or two recent instances where such operations are known to have been conducted on a large scale and review the actual events in connection with such operations. The classical example and the one likely to remain so for as long as any of us will have any interest in the matter is, perhaps, the "pegging" of the sterling rate at $4.76⁷⁄₁₆ for three solid years between the opening months of 1916 and the middle of March of 1919. Ten years further along we have the "stabilizing" operations carried on by the French government precedent to the return of the franc to a gold basis in June of 1928. Finally, much is to be learned from the events in connection with Britain's titanic yet futile struggle to "save the pound" during the summer of 1931.

The now historic "pegging" operation by which the British government held the rate for sterling motionless at ten cents under its par value from the spring of 1916 till the spring of 1919 differs from the others in that it was made possible only by the coöperation of the two governments concerned. Alone, and in the face of her great purchases of materials in the United States, Britain could not possibly have accomplished the holding of the rate. For the way in which her financial representatives in New York remained able during that long period of three years to absorb all offerings of sterling, one thing and one thing only was responsible, and that was the fact that the American Government itself was furnishing the money. England was our ally, needed to buy supplies here, and it was of the utmost importance that the purchasing power of the pound should be sustained. Constantly, then, as the dollar fund with which the British were buying all offerings of sterling bills was drawn down, replenishment took place through fresh advances from the

U. S. Treasury. It was Britain's job to see to it that sterling kept up. It was our job to furnish the money necessary to do it. What the whole operation finally resolved into was a test as to whether the United States Government could and would put up enough money to see the thing through. The answer is that it did, and that it was not until the War had been over for six months and until the advances from the U. S. Treasury had come to an end, that the rate was allowed to break and seek its naturally lower level.

Operations Incident to Reëstablishment of the Franc

The story of the French Government's operations in the exchange market preceding the return to a gold basis of the franc in 1928 is entirely different. There was then no national emergency, no obligation whatever on our part to coöperate with the French Government in the carrying out of its financial plans. The exchange rate on Paris having after November of 1926 settled down to a more or less steady level of just below four cents per franc, the French Government became anxious to get the franc back on a gold basis at around that level and set about making its preparations to do so. This time of course, as when the franc along with the pound had been "stabilized" during the War, no active coöperation was to be expected from the American Government. If France wanted her currency back on a gold basis at four cents per franc or any other figure, that was a matter entirely for the French fiscal authorities to handle.

How excellent a job they made of it, how correct was their judgment as to the level at which permanent stabilization could be accomplished, is shown by the fact that never once after November of 1926 did the monthly average exchange rate for francs go lower than 3.91 or higher than 3.96 cents per franc. There were times of course when the agents here of the Bank of France had to step in and buy heavily in order to keep the rate from going down and there were other times when francs had to be offered freely to keep the rate from getting away on the up side. At no time, however, did the situation threaten to get out of control. Never, it is believed (though on this point as no figures are given out it is impossible to be sure), did the amount of franc drafts which the Bank had to buy run to a figure which threatened the ultimate success of the operation. Very deliberately and very accurately had the French authorities gauged the level at which the franc, stabilized at first by government purchases and sales of bills, could be made convertible into gold and allowed to stand on its own feet.

As a matter of fact, from the size of the balances of the Bank of France in New York at the end of the operation by which in June of 1928 the franc was put back on a gold basis, it is perfectly plain that the amount of franc exchange which the Bank had to buy was considerably less than had been expected. Undoubtedly during the course of the operation there were times when the Bank had to step in and buy on a substantial scale; but, judging from the net result in the way of dollar balances at the end of the op-

eration, there must also have been times when in order
to keep the rate down the Bank must have been a
heavy seller. Certainly, from the comparatively narrow range in which purchases and sales were made,
there can have resulted no very heavy gain or loss—
a condition very different from that attending the
operation which we shall next attempt to describe.

The Battle for the Pound

In a previous chapter dealing with the foreign balances maintained by Central Banks, there was outlined the series of events leading up to Britain's great
effort to hold the pound as against the dollar and the
franc in the summer of 1931. The virtual "trapping"
of a huge sum of British short term capital in the
German market had, it will be recalled, resulted in
a frightened "run" on London by French depositors
there. So great then became the pressure upon sterling
and the resulting outflow of gold that it became necessary for Britain to go the limit in the way of utiliz-
ing her every resource in the support of the pound.

Coöperating with the British Government to avert
what it was realized would rock the financial world to
its very foundations, France and the United States,
in a series of advances, put at the disposal first of the
Bank of England and then of the British Treasury
various amounts of money which finally reached the
huge total of $650,000,000. First the Federal Reserve
Bank here and the Bank of France jointly loaned the
Bank of England $250,000,000. That amount prov-
ing insufficient, a further advance of $400,000,000
was made, direct to the British Treasury, this time

not by the Federal Reserve or the Bank of France, but by private banking interests in America and in France. The French half of this four hundred million dollar loan was made in equal proportions by a syndicate of Paris banks and through an issue of British Treasury bills sold direct to the French public. The American part was contributed by a nation-wide group of banks headed by J. P. Morgan & Co.

With these funds at their disposal the British fiscal authorities went to work, as they had in 1916 and again in 1925, when the pound was put back on a gold basis, to hold the rate. Operating unostentatiously and as much under cover as possible (though everyone of course knew that government buying was going on) the financial agents of the British Government saw to it that all substantial offerings of sterling found a buyer. No attempt of course was made, as had been the case during the War, to peg the sterling rate at any given figure. Rather it was sought, by the judicious placing of supporting orders, to keep the market in so healthy a stage as to stave off, to the greatest extent possible, offerings of exchange by those who from fear or any other cause might be tempted to sell. If only the market can be kept within bounds, it was felt, the incentive to dispose of sterling will be largely done away with. When those with balances in London realize that we intend to hold the rate and that we have the money to do it, they will make up their minds to leave their balances where they are and stop drawing and offering their sterling bills.

That was the theory. In practice, however, things worked out very differently. Instead of figuring that with the British Government provided with so great a sum of money the exchange rate was perfectly safe, holders of sterling seemed from the very beginning to feel that a situation requiring such heroic measures was not one in which they cared to repose their confidence. So, almost as soon as the first advance of $250,000,000 had been made, offerings of sterling, which it had been felt would be greatly reduced, began actually to increase. Instead of the British financial agents being able, as they had figured they would be able, to sell out on rallies the exchange they were having to buy for purpose of support, they found themselves almost continuously on the buying side.

Of strength in the market there was none. It was a case of buy, buy and keep on buying—and even then of seeing quotations almost always at the lower level of the zone in which it was imperative that they be held.

Within three weeks after the first advance of a quarter of a billion dollars to the Bank of England, that institution's buying power became virtually exhausted and a second advance, this one of four hundred million dollars, was made direct to the British Treasury. Thereafter sterling showed some signs of rallying, but almost immediately there developed the same old condition of an apparently endless offering of bills. For a time the British agents stuck to their guns and held the line. Then, it becoming apparent that the amount of bills for sale had been greatly underestimated, the Treasury ceased buying, the market broke wide open and, on September 21, England went off the gold standard.

How much the unsuccessful attempt to hold the sterling rate cost the British Government has never been divulged. On the face of it, considering the sum involved and the fact that the break in sterling when it came amounted to over 25%, the amount must have been large. How large of course depends upon what proportion of the second credit was actually used in the attempt to hold the rate. Very possibly when, in the first weeks of September, it became apparent how overwhelmingly large were the offerings of exchange, the Treasury held back and did not throw its full strength into the breach. Very possibly when it became apparent that the original line could not be held, the Treasury decided to conserve its buying power for stabilizing operations at the new low level whatever it might be. Be that as it may, the sterling bought up around par and subsequently sold a dollar or more in the pound cheaper must have cost the British Government an enormous amount. That, where the stakes are large and the game is lost, is bound to be the case.

"Equalization Fund" Operations

The three instances of direct government interference with the exchange markets outlined above are valuable perhaps for what they show under certain circumstances can actually happen. In all three cases, however, it must be borne in mind, the circumstances were decidedly unusual. A government wishing to stabilize an exchange rate and deciding to utilize its resources to do so, is not often called upon to face such conditions as the British Treasury was called upon to face in 1916 and again in 1931. The regulation of an exchange rate between two countries is inevitably an operation involving large amounts of money; but on the other hand, is by no means necessarily the titanic task faced by the British during the War or a dozen years later when the financial collapse of Central Europe rocked the world's markets to their very foundations. Government intervention in the exchange markets can be and, indeed, usually is, of a far less spectacular character. Very quietly, as a general thing, the financial agents of governments go about their buying and selling and in such a way that, while the end sought is actually being accomplished, the means used are not visible.

There has just been voted by the British Parliament, as this is written, an "Exchange Equalization Fund" amounting to £150,000,000. That such a sum was voted had, of course, to be made public; but as to the purpose for which it is to be used, as to the way in which it is to be administered, no information has been given out and the chances are that none ever will. The Fund, presumably, will be absorbed into the regular operations of the Bank and, in all probability, before a great length of time, will cease to attract any attention whatsoever. When, however, the British Government feels the necessity of stabilizing some rate or, possibly, of "helping" some rate seek a higher or a lower level, the wherewithal will be at hand. To the outside world the means used will not be visible—the outside world will in all probability never even realize that means *are* being used—but the results desired will be none the less surely accomplished.

Control of Exchange through Control of Money Rates

There have been described in the preceding paragraphs what may be called the two obvious forms of government intervention in exchange affairs: the first through open regulation of merchandise exports and imports, and the second through direct purchases and sales of bills. We come now to a third form of intervention, none the less effective but far more subtle. Restriction of the merchandise movement and direct manipulation of rates may be likened to the use of the broadsword and the battleax. The fine Italian touch, the use of the rapier, is seen when a government operates to control a rate of exchange not by methods so blunt and visible, but by indirection, by influencing those conditions which themselves influence the rate of exchange.

In an earlier part of our study we saw to what a very great extent, in anything like normal times, exchange rates are affected by the rate for money. We saw how, when interest rates at any important center tend to rise, exchange rates on that point tend also to rise by reason of the natural desire to send money to any market where a greater return can be had for its use. Conversely, we saw how, when interest rates go down, exchange rates on that point are lowered through the withdrawal of loanable capital which inevitably takes place. As a determinant of exchange rates, it is plain, money rates are a factor of the very first importance. Control the rate for money, it may almost be said, and, as between two markets in anything like a normal condition, you control the rate of exchange.

Government control of money rates, through its control of Central Bank policy, is very great indeed. Where conditions in a country are such that money is in great supply or demand and interest rates are consequently low or high, a government cannot, of course, arbitrarily change the level of rates overnight. Given a little time, however, a government can, even under such conditions, by reason of its ability to contract or to expand credit through the operations of its Central Bank, gradually raise or lower the level of money rates as it sees fit. Very positive and definite indeed, as we shall see, are the means at the disposal of a government for the control of the money market.

Central Bank Policy—The Discount Rate

The first of these, the most powerful weapon of them all, is the ability arbitrarily to raise and lower the official discount rate.

We shall in the following paragraphs be so frequently referring to the official discount rate, the bank rate, as it is frequently called, that it will be well perhaps to pause for a moment and make sure that we quite understand what the bank-rate is. Essentially of course there is no difference between the term "discount rate" as applied to the operation of a Central Bank and as applied to the operations of any other bank. It is a fact, nevertheless, and a most important one, that whereas the rate at which a private bank discounts a bill is a matter of individual negotiation and subject to daily and indeed almost hourly change, the rate at which a government Central Bank does its discounting is a rate definitely fixed and officially stated once every week. The "private" or "open market" rate, that is to say the rate at which the private banks will discount a bill, is constantly changing; the "public rate," that is to say the rate at which bills can be discounted at the Central Bank, is one previously fixed and announced and one which, under ordinary circumstances, is allowed to stand unchanged for months on end. The "open market" rate, it is to be borne in mind, applies to the regular transactions between the private banks and their customers; the "bank-rate" to the rate at which the Central Bank re-discounts paper brought to it by the private banks.

What then is the relation of the open market rate to the bank-rate? Simply this, that the bank-rate goes a long way toward determining, within limits, what the open market rate is to be. A private bank which discounts a bill for a customer does so with full knowledge of the fact that, before the bill runs off, it may itself want to take that same bill around to the Central Bank and get it re-discounted. That being the case, it is plain, no bank is going to discount a bill for a customer at a rate very much lower than the official rate which it knows it will itself have to pay at the Central Bank in case re-discounting of the bill becomes advisable or necessary. A slightly lower rate perhaps, yes—particularly if money is easy and the bank feels that the chances of its ever wanting to re-discount the bill are slight. But, competition or no competition, not too much under the official bank-rate. To do so is to take too much of a chance. There is no nourishment in discounting a bill at say two percent, and later having to get it re-discounted at perhaps three.

Objection will perhaps be made to the above statement that the bank-rate largely influences the open market rate, and the fact pointed out that on innumerable occasions in the past the raising or lowering of the bank-rate has followed and not preceded strength or weakness in rates in the open market. That, it is true, when the Central Bank has no particular interest in the level of rates one way or the other is indeed the case, but it is not conditions such as these that are at present under discussion. What we are inquiring into is not the general relation of official to open market rates but the question as to whether and how far a Central Bank can, when it desires to do so, influence the general price that is being paid for money. To which of course there is only one answer: that whether we are speaking of the Federal Reserve or the Bank of England or any other Central Bank, any one of these institutions can, through its ability arbitrarily to raise or to lower the official rate, exert a very great influence on interest rates in general.

Anything like general discussion of Central Bank policy would, of course, carry us far beyond the limits of a work such as this, but we shall perhaps do well, in passing, to note whence in our own country at least there emanates the great power which goes with the ability to raise and lower the bank-rate. Theoretically, it is true, each of the twelve Federal Reserve Banks is supposed to fix the bank-rate for its own Reserve District, but to imagine that in practice rates in the various Districts are raised and lowered without regard to the rates prevailing in other districts or to other outside financial conditions, would be a very great mistake. The fact being that no regional rate *can* be raised or lowered without the consent of the Federal Reserve Board in Washington, it will readily appear to what an important degree the Secretary of the Treasury, the Comptroller of the Currency and their six associates figure in the matter. Especially in the case of such districts as New York, Boston and Philadelphia, while it might perhaps be going too far to say that action as to the bank-rate originates in Washington, it is certainly a fact that nothing important is ever done except in coöperation with the Reserve Board. Which, no doubt, is as it should be. There must, after all, in a matter of such very great importance to the business of the entire nation be a centralized authority, and that authority in this case is logically the Federal Reserve Board at Washington and no one else. On one or two occasions—notably in 1928 when the New York Bank wanted the rate raised and the Washington Board didn't—there have been clashes of wills, but most of the time the prevailing system of centralized authority has worked exceedingly well.

Central Bank Policy—Other Effects

The raising or lowering of an official discount rate, it must be borne in mind, has important effects other than those exerted on the rate of exchange with foreign countries. Before, then, a bank-rate is altered in order to influence a rate of exchange, full consideration is given to the question as to what are likely to be the effects of such action in other directions. It is of course easier to hit a given mark with a shotgun than with a rifle; but, under some circumstances, a shotgun cannot be used. Take a case for example, where on account of withdrawals of foreign capital, the exchange rate is hovering around the gold export point and gold in unpleasant amounts is beginning to go out. A sharp mark-up in the bank-rate might, it is true, depress the rate of exchange and stop the gold outflow, but such action might also, it is equally true, have unpleasant effects which would more than offset any advantage thus to be gained. The bond market for instance might be unfavorably affected, and this perhaps at a time when the Government itself was about to come into the market for a loan. Business sentiment, moreover, might be adversely influenced by the fear of a coming period of higher money rates and general contraction of credit. Some of the slugs from the shotgun, in other words, might easily fly past the target and do a lot of harm.

The raising or lowering of an official bank-rate, then, is a ticklish piece of business and one rightly entrusted only to an authority in a position to see the situation as a whole and to strike a balance between the possible favorable and unfavorable aspects of the action contemplated. That this power has consistently in our own case been wisely used is proved by the minimum of criticism that has attended the acts of the Federal Reserve Board. So far at least politics has been kept out of Reserve Bank policy and the country has come to realize that when the bankrate is raised or lowered such action is taken because, and solely because, in the opinion of the authority best qualified to judge, the general financial interest of the country will best be served thereby. The Federal Reserve Board at Washington, be it remembered, is in an exceptional position to judge what financially is for the good of the country as a whole. Its sources of information as to actual conditions in finance and industry are not only accurate and complete but, in addition to that, there is the fact that the Chairman of each of the twelve Reserve Banks (the Reserve Agent) is a direct appointee of the Central Board at Washington and is in constant touch with that body. Any policy decided on by the Board at Washington is, thus, by no means a mere expression of opinion on the part of a body aloof from the actual scene of operations, but represents in fact the considered judgment of the Board on the facts as presented by the various Reserve Agents. On such a matter, therefore, as for instance whether the condition of the exchange market calls for a change in the official discount rate at New York, the Board at Washington is in a far better and more detached position to render judgment than any local board of bankers and business men could possibly be. If the shotgun is to be used, to return once more to our old metaphor, it is well that the shooting should be entrusted to someone in a position to judge all possible effects.

The London Bank-rate

So much for the discount rate in New York. How about London—is the bank-rate there a more or a less effective weapon of credit policy than it is here? An exchange rate, we have seen, is a two-ended thing and, like a seesaw, subject to pressure applied at both ends. The Bank of England in London and the Federal Reserve in America each have the power to raise and lower discount rates. By the action of which body is the exchange rate affected to the greater degree?

The answer is that the much greater centralization of banking power in England gives the London bank-rate a degree of effectiveness far beyond that of our own. Where in the United States the banking strength of the country is distributed literally among thousands of banks, in England it is concentrated largely in a group of institutions which can be numbered on the fingers of one hand. Each of the London "Big Five" banks, it is true, has a very large number of branches, but that in no wise alters the fact that general banking policy in each case is a matter for Head Office decision. It is not in England, in other words, as it is here, with thousands of separately owned institutions each entirely independent of the other. There can exist in London, in consequence, and generally does, a unanimity of thought and opinion on banking matters entirely unknown in the United States.

There exists in London, moreover, a much closer relationship between the banks and the Central Bank than is the case here—if, indeed, the Federal Reserve can be called a Central Bank. For well over a century the Bank of England—the Old Lady of Threadneedle Street—has held undisputed her position as matriarch of the British banking family. Here, of course, we have nothing like that, the Federal Reserve System having been brought into existence less than a score of years ago. Ably managed as it has been from the beginning, the Federal Reserve has, therefore, as yet had no chance to build up a relationship with the private banks in any way comparable to that existing between the Bank of England and the privately operated British institutions. While roughly two-thirds of the banking power of the United States is today included in the Federal Reserve System, two-thirds of the total number of banks in the country yet remain outside. That, of course, is a state of affairs very different from that prevailing in England, where from time immemorial The Bank has been a tradition, an acknowledged leader in the banking thought of the country.

When therefore the British bankrate, for the purpose of correcting the exchange or for any other reason, is raised or lowered, a maximum degree of cooperation on the part of the British banks is invariably experienced. When, for example, too much short term foreign capital is coming into the London market and the directors of the Bank decide to lower the bankrate in order to discourage the inflow, they can rest assured that everything will be done by the big private institutions to make the further deposit of outside funds in the London market at least temporarily unattractive. Again, if it is felt that the market is leaning too heavily on the Bank and the rate is raised to discourage further borrowings, the private banks will be quick to adopt a policy of letting the bills in their portfolios run off and of recalling the funds loaned to bill brokers. It is not as in this country a case of "many men many minds"—with a considerable proportion of them holding to their own ideas as to what should be done and acting accordingly. It is a case there of following, without question, a long-trusted leadership.

Another thing, naturally, which gives to the British bank-rate an efficaciousness greater than that possessed by our own is the fact that the bill market in London is larger, more sensitive and far more highly organized than it is in New York. To the American banker the "acceptance"—the bill accepted by a bank —is a new phase of banking practice. To the British banker it is the one way of doing business he has known all his life. To anything then, a raised or lowered bank-rate, for example, which bears directly on the bill market, there is accorded a degree of importance in London which we, on this side, find it perhaps difficult to understand. The bank acceptance, "the bill," in London, is the backbone of the banking system. In this country it occupies no such position.

Federal Reserve Bank Policy

Our survey of the discount rate and its functions, we shall find, will be incomplete unless we at least note also in passing those "open market operations" of the Federal Reserve Bank with which the raising and lowering of the bank-rate are almost invariably so closely connected. Wanting to make money rates easy (usually in preparation for a lowering of the bank-rate and in order to make such action more effective) the Reserve Bank can go into the market and buy government bonds, the money so disbursed being made available for loaning by the banks. Wanting to tighten money rates, the Reserve, on the other hand, can sell its holdings of "governments," the money it receives in payment being thus taken out of the market. Always in a position to conduct such operations on a scale running into the hundreds of millions, either on the buying or selling side, the Reserve System, it will be readily apparent, is armed with an instrument of tremendous efficacy for expanding or contracting the available credit supply as it sees fit.

Again avoiding the danger of letting our examination of the Reserve Bank's power to influence exchange rates run off into a general discussion of Reserve Bank credit policy, it will be well, nevertheless, to point out how on many occasions the "open market operations" in government bonds above referred to become an integral part of the raising or lowering of the discount rate. A time comes, we will say, when, with credit in too free supply, money rates in New York have fallen to a low point, with the result that foreign capital on deposit here is being withdrawn on a great scale. To correct that condition an advance in the bank-rate is of course the logical move but, quite possibly, at the very time of which we are speaking, the banks are out of debt to the Reserve to such a degree that a mere advance in the bankrate would have little effect one way or the other. An advance in the bank-rate is what is really necessary and what will do the business, but, before such a move is undertaken, a certain amount of preparation is needed to make it effective.

What then quite probably happens is that the Reserve Bank begins selling out of its holdings of government bonds. Who does the buying makes little difference. As the bonds are sold, checks drawn on member banks are tendered in payment and the amount of such checks are debited to the member bank's account at the Reserve. Under the necessity, then, of keeping intact its deposit, the member bank will, in all probability start re-discounting some of its holdings of bills at the Reserve Bank or selling the bills outright, which, of course, amounts to the same thing. With the technicalities of the operation we need not trouble ourselves too much. What is important is that as a consequence of the selling of government bonds by the Reserve Bank a very considerable amount of money is drawn out of the open market into the Bank, with the result that, the available supply of funds being thus diminished, interest rates tend to rise. Which, of course, is the "preparation" before referred to. The over-supply of funds having been thus mopped up and the banks having been thus forced into a condition of indebtedness at the Reserve Bank, the effect of an increase in the bank-rate is rendered much more potent. With the banks heavily committed at the Reserve, the effect of such an increase is inevitably to cause curtailment of accommodation, calling of loans and, in fact a general tightening of the reins of credit. Higher rates for money follow as a natural result.

The other side of the picture is where the Reserve Bank, desiring to make open market rates easier, goes into the open market and *buys* government bonds. Here again it makes no difference from whom the buying is done, the net result of the operation, stripped of its technicalities, being that very considerable supplies of loanable capital are released by the Bank for the use of the market. What happens then is that the banks, if they happen at the time to be in debt to the Reserve, take the money they receive from the the sale of the bonds, use it to pay off their loans, and get themselves into a position to extend accommodation much more freely to their regular customers. Money rates, under the circumstances are bound to go down.

If there remains any question as to the ability of the Federal Reserve to conduct bond-buying and selling operations of a magnitude sufficient to bring about the results noted above, a glance at the actual figures on some of the major operations conducted during the past ten years should be sufficient to convince the most skeptical. Between January and May of 1922, for example, the Federal Reserve System bought $400,000,000 of government securities. During the following year—June, 1922, to July 1923—sales amounted to $525,000,000. Again, between December 1923 and September 1924, the Reserve released to the market no less than $510,000,000 through the purchase of government bonds. And so on and so on. As this is being written (the spring of 1932) the Reserve Bank has in the short space of four weeks purchased close to half a billion dollars of government bonds and no end to the movement is as yet in sight. Marvellously well equipped, apparently, is the Reserve System to pour loanable funds into the money market or to take them out.

CHAPTER IX

THE GOLD STANDARD

WHAT *is* the gold standard and what today is the status of the gold standard among the currency systems of the world? What happens to force a country off the gold standard and after it has been forced off what happens in a country's internal financial affairs? How, after a country has gone off the gold standard, are its commercial and financial relationships with other countries affected? What, finally, is the process of return to a gold basis?

The above are the questions with which this chapter has to deal.

Gold, the Common Measure of Value

In the economic development of nations various articles have at various times served as "money," as the common measure of value. In the early days of our country, among the colonists of Virginia, a fixed amount of tobacco was used as the medium of exchange. Cattle among the early Greeks and Romans, slaves in certain parts of Africa and Asia, long constituted the measure of the value of goods and services. Always among peoples emerging from the stage of the pure barter of one article for another, there has developed this need of a financial yardstick, of something in the terms of whose value the value of every-

187

thing else could be expressed. And always, be it noted, the article thus chosen as a medium of exchange has itself been an article of definite value to the people so using it. Diomedes selling his Ægean villa for ten sleek bullocks or Jones of Jamestown selling his boat for a hogshead of tobacco, may not have intended to keep the bullocks or the tobacco, but parted with the house and the boat, nevertheless, only for something whose future value was definitely assured.

Later, as economic progress was made and the need increased for a medium of exchange of greater usability, the metals, particularly the precious metals, came generally to be adopted for this purpose. Silver for a long time remained the favorite but finally, except in the Orient, came to be superseded by the most suitable metal of all, gold. In 1816 England adopted gold as its sole standard and one by one the other nations of the Occident fell into line. With the great industrial awakening in the middle of the last century it came to be realized that it was of the utmost importance that all nations doing business together should have the same medium of exchange, and that, for that purpose, nothing known could surpass the suitability of gold.

Suitability of Gold as a Medium of Exchange

Not the least of the reasons for the suitability of gold as a medium of exchange is the ease with which it lends itself to standardization, to coinage into pieces of a definite weight and fineness (degree of purity). Gold having been adopted as the medium of exchange, each nation was in a position to decree what weight of gold and of what fineness should constitute its monetary unit. England said, Our monetary unit shall be the sovereign and shall contain 7.9881 grams of gold 91.66% pure. The United States said, Our monetary unit shall be the dollar and shall contain 25.80 grains of gold 90% pure. And so on. Each nation adopting gold as its medium of exchange fixed by law the gold content of its monetary unit. The sovereign, then, and the dollar and the others became definite measures of an amount of gold. The fact that a gold coin happened to be marked "One sovereign" or "Ten dollars" wasn't the important thing. The important thing was that the man possessing one or more of these coins, so marked by a responsible government, was in a position to know exactly of how much gold he was the owner. When, for instance, he parted with something of value in exchange for a disc of metal marked "Ten dollars" he knew that he was getting 258 grains, plus, of gold, nine-tenths pure.

The coining of gold then really represents nothing more nor less than the putting up of gold into a convenient and standardized package. Any kind of piece of gold of any size or shape would really do just as well but would simply be less convenient. Every time a piece of gold passed from buyer to seller it would be necessary to verify its weight and to subject it to a more or less complicated metallurgical test. Through the coining of gold all that is avoided. The government weighs it, tests it and stamps it. By everyone thereafter it is realized that no further weighings or testings are necessary. By which, of

course, the usability of gold as a medium of exchange
is very greatly increased.

"As Good as Gold"

Among civilized nations adopting gold as their
standard of value, it soon became apparent that anything that could at any time be exchanged for one of
these definite amounts of gold, one of these coins,
was as good or even a better medium of exchange than
the coins themselves. Gradually, then, it began to be
realized that the promise of a responsible party—of a
government, for example, or a great bank—to pay
gold, was just as good as the gold itself and far more
convenient to handle. Various other forms of "money"
thereupon began to come into existence, some of them
promises to pay issued by governments, some of them
promises to pay issued by banks under close government restriction and supervision. Always, however,
immediate convertibility into gold was the important
consideration. Only as long as everybody knew that
this "paper" could instantly at the option of the holder
be exchanged for coin, would it circulate on a par with
coin as a medium of exchange.

It has been considered advisable to re-state the former perhaps rather elementary facts because only by
holding these principles firmly in mind can we get the
true picture of what the Gold Standard really is and
of how it came into existence. Needing a medium of
exchange more usable than the original herds of cattle,
the slaves and the hogsheads of tobacco, civilized
mankind turned first to gold and then to paper con-

vertible into gold. Always, however, the principle was maintained that the thing selected as the yardstick of value must itself have definite and intrinsic value. Pieces of paper, promises to pay, alongside of the gold coin itself—yes. But only as long as the issue of those pieces of paper, of those promises to pay, was regulated in such a manner as to leave no possible question that the man holding them could, at any time he so desired, turn them into the gold metal itself.

What the Gold Standard Means

Very simply then the term "gold standard" means the instant convertibility into gold coin of every form of legally issued "money." A country in which the government stands ready instantly to redeem in gold any and all of its own notes or those of its Central Bank, is on a gold basis. It is on a gold basis no longer when there is imposed any restriction whatsoever on the full payment in gold of its demand obligations.

What about a country which pays its notes in gold but which prohibits exports of the metal—can such a country be said to be on a gold basis? Nominally, perhaps, but certainly in no true sense of the term. By the embargo on exports, it is true, the right of its own citizens to convert their notes into gold is not abridged; but how about the holdings of those living outside the country and desiring to repatriate their funds? They, too, it is a fact, can convert their bank deposits into notes and their notes into gold, but what are they going to do with the gold after their agents have received it? They have funds on deposit here which they wish to bring back to their own country and that they are prevented from doing. Is it not a fact then that the gold embargo cuts them off from the use of what is rightfully theirs? And if that is the case and the payment of the notes they present is accomplished only with such restrictions that they cannot get actual possession of their funds, can the claim rightly be made that the country stands ready to redeem its obligations in gold—in other words, that the gold standard is in full effect? It would hardly seem so. The very essence of the gold standard principle being that bank deposits (through conversion into government or government-bank currency) can at any time be withdrawn in the form of gold, a condition of affairs where the depositor is paid and then prohibited from taking his money away would seem a gross violation of that principle. No government is truly on the gold standard basis unless the holder of its notes, wherever he may happen to reside, can at any time he wishes convert those notes into gold and do with the gold as he sees fit. By any qualification whatsoever the principle of the gold standard is completely vitiated.

Recognition of the above is of the utmost importance in any attempt to figure where the gold standard currently stands among the currencies of the world. There are to-day, as a matter of fact, just five countries which are truly on the gold standard, the United States of America, France, Switzerland, Belgium and Holland. In those countries, and in those countries only, government and government-bank notes exchange instantly for the amount of gold they call for and no restrictions whatever, "moral" or otherwise, exist as to the export and import of the precious metal. In every other country in the world either the exchange of notes for gold has been suspended or, where such exchange has not been suspended, export and import restrictions exist.

The Gold Standard To-day

Without venturing on to the highly controversial subject as to whether the gold standard is or is not the ideal monetary system, this may be said, that no first rank country has ever voluntarily gone off the gold basis and that every country which through force of circumstances *has* been forced off gold, has moved heaven and earth to get back on it again. We ourselves went off just before the end of the War when in September of 1917 the Federal Reserve Board placed an embargo on gold exports, but went back on again almost immediately after the Armistice, although our doing so caused us to lose an immense amount of gold to the Orient and to South America. England began her preparations as soon as the War was over and resumed the gold standard in 1925. France followed suit three years later. Always, we see, there has existed this same determination on the part of every first rank power to get on and remain on the gold basis if humanly possible.

If it is argued that conditions have changed, that the world's supply of gold has become inadequate, that the gold standard is no longer the logical monetary system, the reply may with truth be made that after every upheaval during the past half century we have heard the same thing. Innumerable schemes running all the way from "managed currencies" to a monetary unit based on the fluctuation of commodity prices have been proposed and economically sponsored and solemnly discussed; but always it has come back to this, that the gold standard, while admittedly far from perfect, has been proved to be by far the most workable system that has ever been devised. The United States on the gold standard, France on the gold standard, England's Chancellor almost as this is written avowing his country's intention to return to gold at the earliest possible moment—no, the system which for the past century has stood the civilized world so well, is apparently still far from being superseded by any of these economists' dreams.

"Off the Gold Standard"

What, after all, happens in a country which, in accordance with or against its will, abandons the gold standard? What but a greater or lesser degree of repudiation of that government's solemn obligations? A country is on the gold basis and its paper passes, as a medium of exchange, on a par with gold. Why? For what other reason than that the people accept at face value the explicit promise of that government that for each dollar or each pound or each franc of its paper, it will pay the holder a definite weight in gold? A weight, remember, not an amount. The ten-dollar Federal Reserve note you have in your pocket states that the United States will pay you ten dollars in gold for it, and the law of the country defines exactly what weight of gold each of those dollars shall contain. When, therefore, a government goes off the gold standard, refuses to exchange your note for gold, leaves you with something on your hands for which you will have to accept a lesser amount of gold than the note calls for, what, after all, is that but actual repudiation? In what essential way, as a matter of fact, is it any different than if, as a holder of a government bond come due, you presented it for payment and were told that the bond would not be paid?

That, gentle reader, who has perhaps been thinking lightly about this business of "going off the gold standard," is the first thing that happens. The next is that all debts are by such action automatically scaled down to the extent that the paper money of the country depreciates in comparison with gold. You are an Englishman, we will say, and someone owes you a hundred pounds sterling, in other words, 732.24 grams of fine gold—which gold you are free to turn into money in England or the United States or any country you choose. England "goes off the gold standard" and the paper pound depreciates, perhaps, 25%. You are still, it is true, owed one hundred pounds, but are you still owed 732.24 grams of fine gold? Hardly. You may be *owed* 732.24 grams of gold but what you are going to *get* is 25% less grams, in other words, 548.18 grams. You are thinking perhaps of going to the United States or of investing in some American security. What your 732.24 grams of gold would have secured for you in the way of American dollars was $486.65. What the 548.18 grams you actually get will secure for you is $364.33.

That is all very true, it may be objected, with regard to the purchasing power of the hundred pounds in some foreign market, but is it not a fact that at home the hundred pounds will buy just as much as they ever would? Admitting a reduction of 25% (or whatever the gold premium happens to be) in their purchasing power as applied to American securities, is it not still a fact that the hundred paper pounds will in England exchange for as great an amount of life's necessities as was the case before they became nonconvertible into gold?

The answer is that that is a question not of whether the country is or is not on a gold basis, but purely a question of whether the amount of outstanding inconvertible paper money is or is not increased. If after a country abandons the gold standard it refrains from issuing additional paper currency, there is no reason whatever why there should be any change in the level of commodity prices. If, on the other hand, the government printing presses are set to work, commodity prices are bound to rise. Theoretically, even so, the actual cost of living will not go up because everyone is supposed to come into possession of that much more of the additional currency, but in actual practice the distribution of the newly printed money is exceedingly uneven and a great deal of hardship invariably results.

Effect on Commodity Prices

The prevailing idea, of course, that when a country goes off the gold basis commodity prices immediately begin to rise, is due to the world's painful remembrance of what happened in Germany and France and other Continental European countries just after the end of the War. Off the gold standard and no longer under the necessity of redeeming their notes in gold, the governments of those countries turned the printing presses to work and poured out floods of new currency. The result was that commodity prices, in terms of that currency, went sky high—in the case of Germany to a level where the cost of many articles of little intrinsic value rose into the billions of marks. France, it is true, and Italy, after satisfying the needs of the government by the issue of some scores of billions of paper francs and lire, stopped far short of the point at which the currency would become worthless; but, as it was, prices in those countries rose to fantastic heights. All over Europe it was the same thing—the outstanding paper currency being doubled and doubled again, and the price of everything being advanced correspondingly.

That then is the picture which the world has in mind as to what happens in a country when it goes off the gold standard. That the picture can, however, be very different, is proved by what happened in England after the forced abandonment of the gold standard in September of 1931. Following the news that the Bank of England had stopped redeeming its notes in gold, it was everywhere expected that the paper currency would be largely increased, that prices of stocks and commodities would begin to rise—that, in fact, the entire familiar drama of currency inflation and its inevitable consequences were once more about to be reënacted. That, however, is just exactly what did not happen. From a level of 107.8 on September 30, 1931, the sterling index of commodity prices rose in six weeks to 110.3, but, when it became evident that there was to be no ballooning of the currency, came to a definite halt. Eight months later, as this is written, with the note circulation of the Bank at almost exactly the same figure at which it stood when gold was abandoned, the level of commodity prices in Britain shows an actual decline of some 4%.

In dealing with this question of the gold standard, it is very plain then that generalizations are, as usual, unsafe and misleading, and it is vastly important that the facts in each particular case be taken into consideration. Germany deliberately debasing her currency to a state of worthlessness in order to wipe out all debts payable in the old mark and England, temporarily driven off the gold standard, fighting valiantly to get back on again and live up to her agreements are, it is evident, two entirely different propositions. There are, in other words, ways and ways for a country to go off the gold standard and, even more important, to handle its monetary affairs after it has gone off. Possibly, indeed, if we look a little closer at the events attending and following the suspension of the Bank Act, we shall see that while Britain did everything in her power to keep from being thrown off the gold standard, she has not been slow to see that with things as they are today there are certain benefits attending such a condition. And, furthermore, that these advantages may not improbably be made the stepping stones for a return to her former financial pedestal.

We need hardly here review the circumstances leading to the suspension of gold payments in England,

which, in a previous chapter, have been described in
some detail. What, however, we do want to be sure
we quite understand is that Britain went off the gold
basis not for any possible advantage that was to be
gained by such action, but because and solely because
of a command over her gold supply by certain outside
markets which was rapidly forcing her banking system into a decidedly unsecure position. That, in its
monumental battle to save the pound in the summer
of '31, the British Government risked and lost a sum
estimated to exceed half a billion dollars, would in
itself seem to prove that the relinquishing of the gold
standard was anything but a voluntary move. The
fact that the British have made the most of the situation in which they have found themselves does not,
it would seem, in the least prove that they voluntarily
got themselves into such a position. What it would
seem rather to indicate is that, finding themselves
driven off gold, the British fiscal authorities are determined to capitalize the advantages of the position
they are in, with a view to getting themselves back
on the gold standard as soon as possible.

Off the Gold Standard—Effect on Foreign Trade

What are the advantages, from a foreign trade
standpoint, of being off the gold standard?

Primarily, of course, that a depreciated currency, a
not too greatly depreciated currency, is a strong stimulus to export business. A moment's thought will show
why this is so. A merchant in England, for example,
selling goods in the United States or any other foreign
country, does so with the idea of winding up the trans-

action with a profit in his own currency—in sterling and in no other currency than sterling. If he makes the sale in France, it is true, he will get paid in francs, and if he makes it in the United States he will get paid in dollars; but what he is after, none the less, is a profit expressed in the currency in which he runs his business, in other words, in pounds. He may receive actual payment for the goods in francs or in dollars or in any other foreign currency, but until that foreign currency, whatever it happens to be, is converted back into sterling, the transaction is unfinished and the profit unrealized.

If then the francs or the dollars buy a larger amount of sterling than would normally be the case, the profit to the British exporter is correspondingly increased. The shipment, we will say, is to the United States, and the dollar proceeds of the sale amount to $4,860. That, under normal conditions, would mean that the British exporter would actually realize £1000. Suppose now, however, that sterling is depreciated 25% as compared with the dollar, in other words, that the price of the pound in New York is not $4.86 but $3.64. How many pounds now can be bought with $4,860, the dollar proceeds of the merchandise? Thirteen-hundred and thirty-five pounds now instead of one thousand pounds, as formerly.

Is the profit to the exporter increased by the full amount of the increase in the number of pounds which his dollars or his francs will buy? That depends, of course, on what it cost him to produce the goods. If his labor and material costs have stood still, or nearly so, there is no reason why his cost of producing and selling the goods should show any appreciable increase over what it was before his country went off the gold basis and its currency became depreciated. If, on the other hand, as was the case in France and Italy, currency inflation has raised the price of everything, his costs of production in francs or lire are bound to be correspondingly increased. So great indeed may have been the increase in his production cost that even in spite of the fact that his dollars and francs now buy so much more of his own depreciated currency, there may be no money to be made in export sales.

Cost of Production

As a matter of practical fact, what happens when the currency of a great exporting nation like Britain becomes depreciated is not that exporters make tremendous profits on their foreign sales, but rather that, because they are able to sell in the foreign market at a lower price than formerly, the volume of their business is likely to be very greatly increased. Assuming that the currency is depreciated, say 25%, and that there has been no appreciable rise in production costs, it is plain that the exporter suddenly finds himself with a 25% "edge" on his competitors so far as price is concerned. That is to say, of course, on his competitors who are on a gold basis. The others are in just the same position as himself. Assuming equal production costs and equal ability to sell in the foreign market, the question of competitive sales price becomes simply a question of the extent to which the currencies of the various competitors are depreciated. Put foreigner A and foreigner B on the same basis so far as selling, say, in the U. S. A. is concerned, and, if A can send home the proceeds of what he sells at a much lower rate of exchange than B can send home the proceeds of what *he* sells, it is plain that A will be able greatly to undersell B.

It is not, however, to be thought that by going off the gold basis and allowing its currency to depreciate say one-quarter or one-third, a country can immediately lower correspondingly the price at which it can sell goods in the foreign market. It is hardly as simple as that. Take again for purposes of illustration the case of England, whose currency as this is written is at a discount of 25% as compared with American dollars. That, of course, is a great thing for England's export business, but there is another side to it which must also be considered. Before a country like England can *export* manufactured goods she has first to *import* the raw materials, and those imports she has got to pay for with her own depreciated currency. If a given amount of cotton, for instance, cost a Lancashire mill one pound sterling under the old order of things, that same amount of cotton now costs a pound and a quarter. It is all very true that when the cotton is manufactured and sold abroad the British exporter is going to get a pound-and-a-quarter where he used only to get a pound; but if when importing the raw cotton from the United States prior to its manufacture he has to pay 25% more pounds for it, it is plain that he is not coming out so very far ahead on the transaction. To the extent that the sales abroad of a depreciated-currency country consist merely of reëxports of merchandise or produce previously imported, the advantage of the currency-discount are nowhere near what they might be expected to be.

Where a country is in a position to produce and export goods which have not had previously to be imported, the above does not of course apply. Nor is the statement to be taken too literally that because imports of raw materials have to be paid for in the depreciated currency, all the advantage of selling the finished goods abroad in a currency that is at a premium with the exporter's, is necessarily lost. For the pound of cotton which under normal foreign exchange conditions would have cost the Manchester spinner threepence he may, it is true, now have to pay fourpence. When, however, that pound of cotton has been manufactured, it is not going to be sold abroad at the equivalent of any fourpence. It is going to be sold abroad at a good deal more than that. The gain of 25%, then, on the export side of the transaction is going to be figured on a much larger amount of money than the loss of 25% on the import side of the transaction. Suppose, for example, that the cost price of the raw cotton was one pound sterling and that the sales price abroad, after manufacture, was two pounds sterling. The net gain on account of currency depreciation in that case, it is plain, would be one-quarter of one pound sterling, 12½% on the export transaction.

The figures given above are of course merely illustrative and not to be literally taken. They do serve to show, however, the undoubted advantages which accrue to the export trade of a country whose currency is selling at a discount in the outside markets. There is such an advantage, and the first thing that any nation temporarily driven off the gold standard can be counted upon to do is to attempt to capitalize that advantage to the greatest possible extent. In such efforts, indeed, in the building up of a great export trade balance, lies that country's very best chance of regaining control of its normal gold supply and of returning to the gold standard.

Return to Gold

Why, it may at this point well be asked, should a country in the position outlined above *want* to return to the gold standard? The fact that its currency shows some degree of depreciation results, as has been shown, in a country's being able to undersell its erstwhile competitors in foreign markets. Why, under such circumstances, with its export business so stimulated, should a country want to go back to a condition of things when the edge it has on its competitors will at once be completely lost?

The answer very simply is that the foreign trade of a country, of any country, while unquestionably important, by no means necessarily constitutes the dominating consideration. There are other things that have to be taken into account. A currency depreciated in comparison with that of its neighbors results in a country's foreign trade being stimulated, but results in a lot of other things as well. Some of them are not so pleasant. There is a great deal more to this business of going off the gold standard and allowing one's currency to become depreciated than just bringing about a stimulation of one's foreign trade.

First and foremost there is the fact that a gold standard country voluntarily or involuntarily going off gold and refusing to make good on its agreement to pay its paper money in gold, is and remains, until that default is cured, exactly in the position of any other defaulting debtor. There may be reasons in the case of a government as in the case of an individual why the obligation cannot be met, but that in no wise alters the fact that the obligation was deliberately created, that it exists, and that it is not being taken care of. The famous remark that it is impossible to indict a nation is quite true. It is also quite true, however, that a nation with outstanding unredeemed promises to pay, which is not making every possible effort to get itself into a position where it *can* pay, is in just the same position as the individual who owes money and is doing nothing about it.

Aside from any moral consideration, there is plenty of reason why no nation wants to remain long in such a position. Confidence is the very lifeblood of international trade, and confidence, once shaken, takes a long time to restore. Let there be any question of the intention of a country which has had to leave the gold standard to get back to it as soon as possible, and the position of that country in the world's markets becomes highly insecure.

Revaluation of a Currency

What about a country which goes back on the gold standard but on a different basis; which, for instance, again agrees to exchange its paper notes for gold, but for a lesser weight of gold? France, for instance, which in 1928 went back on the gold standard, agreeing to exchange the paper franc for 65.5 milligrams of gold nine-tenths fine as against a previous gold content for the franc of 322.58 milligrams.

How such action can be regarded as other than a sort of composition with one's creditors it is hard to see. A perfectly honorable settlement and, no doubt, the best that could be arranged under the circumstances, its practical effect was none the less a scale-down of 80% in the franc debts owed by the French Government. In order to pay the expenses of the War and those following it, the Government said, we have had to issue a very large amount of paper notes. To pay those notes in gold on demand at the old rate of 322 milligrams per franc is manifestly impossible. Accept an offer to pay 65 milligrams instead, and the notes you hold can be put back on a gold basis. Refuse, and their value will remain as at present indefinite—with always the constant danger that they may further depreciate in relation to gold and that it may thus become necessary to issue further large amounts to pay for current expenses. Small wonder that under the circumstances the holders of French paper currency and of franc bonds were glad to accept the settlement offered them, even though it did involve a write-down of 80%.

Just, however, as different circumstances call for different kinds of settlements among private individuals, so, among nations, the same thing is true. France, for example, staggering under the burden of a fifty-billion franc note issue emitted during and just after the War is an entirely different proposition from

Britain, forced off the gold standard not by any necessitous over-issue of paper money but simply by an unusual combination of circumstances temporarily threatening the Bank of England's gold reserve. For France to have had to settle at "twenty cents on the dollar" was a terrible thing, but something which, if normal conditions were again to be restored, could not be avoided. For Britain to make any "settlement" at less than the 7.33 grams of fine gold per pound sterling provided in the Bank Act would be an entirely different proposition. That weight of gold per pound the holder of a British banknote is entitled to receive and must receive, even though the exigencies of the present situation have made it necessary temporarily to defer the payment.

Meeting the Competition

Again, entirely aside from what might be called the "ethical" reasons above referred to, there is every incentive for a country which has been forced off the gold standard to get back on it again and rejoin the group of nations trading with one another on a basis of fairness and equality. Temporarily, perhaps, a depreciated currency may seem to give a country some slight advantage in the export market, but that advantage is, after all, it is becoming more and more plain, secured at a cost of a good deal more than it is worth. What happens when, on account of depreciation of its currency, a country gets into a position where it can seriously undersell its competitors in some important export market? Almost immediately that there are set up against the products of that country another of those series of quotas, preferentials and tariffs which during the past few years have had such a disastrous effect upon the inter-country movement of the products of industry and enterprise. To no unimportant extent have these barriers been erected in retaliation for what by some nations have been regarded as unfair advantages taken by others. The sooner these practices are done away with, the sooner these barriers are let down, the better it will be for all nations interested in trading with one another. So and so only can there be anything like a resumption of the world trade conditions previously prevailing.

Between Two Depreciated Currencies

What has been said in the above paragraphs about the advantages to export trade of a depreciated currency applies particularly, of course, to trade between gold standard and non-gold standard countries. When, however, we come to the question of trade between two countries both of whose currencies are depreciated, the situation is found not to be so entirely different. The important consideration in that case is the relative amount of depreciation. Two countries doing business together, we will say, have currencies both of which are depreciated as against gold, one to the extent of 25% and the other to the extent of 50%. Other things being equal, the country whose currency is depreciated most has the advantage over the other so far as export business is concerned. To sell in a country whose currency was on a gold basis was, we saw, a great thing for a country whose own currency was depreciated. To sell in a country whose currency, while depreciated in relation to a common standard, is depreciated less than your own is, in effect about the same thing. In both cases the great thing is to be able to take the foreign currency received in payment for the goods and to turn it advantageously into your own money. The more your currency is depreciated, of course, whether in relation to the currency of a gold standard or of a non-gold standard country, the greater will be the amount of your own money which you will be able to secure with the proceeds of your goods.

Gold Still the International Medium of Exchange

Considering that so many countries are now off the gold standard, it is often asked, would it not perhaps be better for the rest of the world to abandon gold at least temporarily so that all countries might be placed on terms of equality? In answering, let us bring into the matter that invaluable thing, a sense of proportion. There are at the present time, it is true, only five countries fully and unrestrictedly on the gold standard, but among those countries we find the U. S. A., which does perhaps one-third of all the business done in the world, and France, another of the world's leading commercial powers. England, furthermore, while at the moment not on a gold basis, is shaping her financial policies along lines which leave no possible room for doubt as to her intentions to return to the gold standard at the earliest possible moment. Right here then, alone, we have three powers, two of them on the gold standard and the other potentially so, doing perhaps seventy-five percent of the world's business. Germany, furthermore, and other important countries, while hampered by necessary gold export restrictions, have kept their monetary systems on a gold basis so that, internally, at least, their currency passes on a parity with gold. Quite an array of countries, it would seem, on the side of the gold standard. Quite an argument, apparently, as to why the gold standard should continue to be maintained.

For after all, as was pointed out at the beginning of this chapter, the gold standard, while admittedly far from perfect, does represent the one and only system which the nations of the world have been able to work out for purposes of mutual financial and commercial intercourse. One country chooses to legislate into existence a thing called the franc, another a thing called the dollar, still another a thing called the pound sterling. As long and only as long as there is a common denominator to which these various currencies can be reduced, can there be a free and unrestricted interchange between them. As long and only as long as the man who owns a franc, a dollar, a pound, knows just exactly what amount of gold he can exchange it for, will he be content to leave his money invested, even temporarily, in the currency of a country other than his own. Without which, of course, there can be no satisfactory financial or commercial relationship among nations.

CHAPTER X

PRINCIPAL MONETARY UNITS OF THE WORLD

ARGENTINA

THE monetary unit of Argentina is the gold peso (plural, pesos) of 100 centavos, representing 1.6129 grams of gold 0.900 fine (1.4516 grams of fine gold). Its par value is $0.9648 United States currency.

AUSTRALIA

Australia's monetary unit is the Australian pound (symbol £) par $4.8665. The metallic currency in circulation is practically the same as in Great Britain.

AUSTRIA

Austria's monetary unit is the schilling (anglicized plural, schillings), of 100 groschen, representing 235.2454 milligrams of gold 0.900 fine (211.72086 milligrams of fine gold), the par value of which is about $0.1407 United States currency.

BELGIUM

The Belgian franc (plural, francs) of 100 centimes, stabilized under the royal decree of October 25, 1926, is the monetary unit of Belgium. The new franc represents 46.491 milligrams of gold 0.900 fine (41.842 milligrams of fine gold), the par value of which is $0.02784 United States currency. The same decree created the belga (plural, belgas), the equivalent of 5 new Belgian francs; it therefore represents 232.457 milligrams of gold 0.900 fine (209.211 milligrams of fine gold), and its par value is $0.1392 United States currency.

BOLIVIA

Bolivia's monetary unit is the boliviano (plural, bolivianos) of 100 centavos, representing 610.19 milligrams of gold 0.900 fine (549.17 milligrams of fine gold), the par value of which is $0.364986 United States currency.

BRAZIL

Theoretically the cruzeiro (of 100 centesimos), a gold coin representing 2 grams of gold 0.900 fine (1.8 grams of fine gold), the par value of which is $1.1963 United States currency, is the monetary unit of Brazil under the law of December 18, 1926, which law provided also that all the paper currency in circulation "be convertible into gold on the basis of 200 milligrams per milreis." This new system, however, has not been fully established and the milreis is still the money of account.

BRITISH INDIA

In British India the monetary unit is the silver rupee (of 16 annas), containing 11.6638 grams (180 grains) of silver 0.916⅔ fine.

British Malaya

STRAITS SETTLEMENTS

In the Crown colony of the Straits Settlements the monetary unit is the Straits dollar of 100 cents, containing 20.2173 grams (312 grains) of silver 0.900 fine.

Bulgaria

Bulgaria's monetary unit is the lev (plural, leva) of 100 stotinki (centimes), representing 12.0773 milligrams of gold 0.900 fine (10.8696 milligrams of fine gold), the par value of which is $0.00722 United States currency.

Canada

The Canadian dollar of 100 cents, representing 1.6718 grams of gold 0.900 fine (1.5046 grams of fine gold), is the exact equivalent of the United States dollar and its par value is the same ($1).

Chile

The monetary unit of Chile is the peso (plural, pesos; symbol, $) of 100 centavos, representing 203.395 milligrams of gold 0.900 fine (183.057 milligrams of fine gold) and having a par value of 6d., or $0.12166 United States currency.

China (SHANGHAI)

The Shanghai tael is the tael in general use in Shanghai, in which foreign exchange rates are quoted by the banks. This tael contains 35.332 grams (545.-25 grains) of silver 0.980 fine. Par in terms of United States dollars varies with the price of silver.

CHINA (HONG KONG)

In the British colony of Hong Kong the monetary unit is the Hong Kong dollar of 100 cents, containing 26.957 grams (416 grains) of silver 0.900 fine. There are also current the British silver dollar, of the same weight and fineness, and the old Mexican dollar, containing 27.07 grams (417.74 grains) of silver 0.9027 fine. The Hong Kong dollar and the British dollar have the same exchange value, but their par of exchange in terms of the United States dollar varies with the price of silver.

CZECHOSLOVAKIA

Czechoslovakia has for its monetary unit the Czechoslovak koruna (plural, koruny) of 100 heller, representing 49.53 milligrams of gold 0.900 fine (44.58 milligrams of fine gold), the new par value of which is $0.0296 United States currency.

DENMARK

Denmark has for its monetary unit the krone (plural, kroner), representing 448.03 milligrams of gold 0.900 fine (403.23 milligrams of fine gold), the par value of which is $0.26798 United States currency.

FINLAND

Finland's monetary unit is the Finnish markka (plural, markkaa) of 100 pennia, representing 42.-

105 milligrams of gold 0.900 fine (37.895 milligrams of fine gold), the par value of which is $0.025185 United States currency.

FRANCE

The new gold French franc (plural, francs) of 100 centimes, representing 65.5 milligrams of gold 0.900 fine (58.95 milligrams of fine gold), the par value of which is $0.039179 United States currency, is the present monetary unit of France. This new unit was adopted in accordance with the stabilization law executed at Paris on June 25, 1928. Prior to that date the unit of currency was the former gold franc representing 322.58 milligrams of gold 0.900 fine, the par value of which was $0.192948.

GERMANY

The monetary unit of the German Republic is the new gold reichsmark (plural, reichsmark; anglicized, reichsmarks) of 100 pfennige, which represents 398.-25 milligrams of gold 0.900 fine (358.42 milligrams of fine gold) and the par value of which is $0.2382 United States currency.

GREECE

The monetary unit of Greece is the drachma (plural, drachmai; anglicized, drachmas) of 100 lepta, representing 21.696 milligrams of gold 0.900 fine (19.526 milligrams of fine gold), the new par value of which is $0.013 United States currency.

Hungary

The monetary unit of Hungary is the pengö (plural, pengö), of 100 filler, representing 292.40 milligrams of gold 0.900 fine (263.16 milligrams of fine gold), the par value of which is $0.1749 United States currency.

Italy

Italy's monetary unit is the lira (plural, lire) of 100 centesimi, stabilized, effective December 22, 1927, at $0.0526315 United States currency. The new lira represents 87.9901 milligrams of gold 0.900 fine (79.-1911 milligrams of fine gold).

Japan

Japan's monetary unit is the yen (plural, yen) of 100 sen, representing 2 fun (750 milligrams) of fine gold—the equivalent of 833.33 milligrams of gold 0.900 fine—the par value of which is $0.4985 United States currency.

Mexico

Mexico's monetary unit is the peso (plural, pesos; symbol, $) of 100 centavos, representing 833.33 milligrams of gold 0.900 fine (750 milligrams of fine gold), the par value of which is $0.4985 United States currency.

Netherlands

For its monetary unit the Netherlands employs the florin (plural, florins), also termed the gulden (plural, gulden), of 100 cents, representing 672 milligrams of gold 0.900 fine (604.8 milligrams of fine gold), the par value of which is about $0.402 United States currency.

NORWAY

Norway's monetary unit is the krone (plural, kroner), representing 448.03 milligrams of gold 0.900 fine (403.23 milligrams of fine gold), the par value of which is $0.26798 United States currency.

PERSIA

Persia's monetary system is based on the silver kran, which weighs about 4.603 grams and is 0.900 fine. There are 20 shahis in a kran, and 10 krans in a toman. The value of the kran in foreign exchange moves with the price of silver.

PHILIPPINE ISLANDS

In the Philippine Islands the monetary unit is the peso (plural, pesos) of 100 centavos, containing 20 grams of silver 0.800 fine and equivalent to $0.50 United States currency.

POLAND

The Republic of Poland has adopted as its monetary unit the zloty (plural, zlote) of 100 grosze. The zloty represents 187.546 milligrams of gold 0.900 fine (168.792 milligrams of fine gold) and is equivalent to about $0.1122 United States currency.

Rumania

The leu (plural, lei) of 100 bani, the gold content of which was fixed at 10 milligrams of gold 0.900 fine (9 milligrams of fine gold) by the stabilization law of February 7, 1929, and the par value of which is $0.00598 United States currency, is the monetary unit of Rumania.

Soviet Russia (U. S. S. R.)

The Union of Socialist Soviet Republics has adopted as its monetary unit the chervonets (plural, chervontsi), equivalent to 10 chervonets rubles. The chervonets ruble is theoretically the exact equivalent of the pre-war Russian ruble (860.26 milligrams of gold 0.900 fine, or 774.234 milligrams of fine gold), and its par value is $0.51455 United States currency.

Spain

The gold peseta (plural, pesetas) of 100 centimos, representing 322.58 milligrams of gold 0.900 fine (290.32 milligrams of fine gold), with a par value the same as that of the former French franc, $0.192948 United States currency, is the monetary unit of Spain.

Sweden

Sweden's monetary unit is the krona (plural, kronor), representing 448.03 milligrams of gold 0.900 fine (403.23 milligrams of fine gold), with a par value of $0.26798 United States currency.

SWITZERLAND

Switzerland has for its monetary unit the Swiss franc of 100 centimes, representing 322.58 milligrams of gold 0.900 fine (290.32 milligrams of fine gold), the par value of which is $0.192948 United States currency.

URUGUAY

Uruguay has for its monetary unit the peso (plural, pesos) of 100 centesimos, representing 1.697 grams of gold 0.9167 fine (1.5273 grams of fine gold), the par value of which is $1.0342 United States currency.

UNITED KINGDOM

The monetary unit of the United Kingdom is the pound sterling of 20 shillings, or 240 pence, representing 7.9881 grams of gold 0.916⅔ fine (7.3224 grams of fine gold), the par value of which is $4.866563523 United States currency but customarily regarded as $4.8665.

YUGOSLAVIA

Yugoslavia employs as its monetary unit the dinar (anglicized plural, dinars) of 100 paras, representing 322.58 milligrams of gold 0.900 fine (290.32 milligrams of fine gold), the par value of which is $0.192948 United States currency.

INDEX

A

Acceptance market in New York, 101, 110.

Arbitrage, theory of, 86; indirect settlements, 86–89; illustration of simple arbitrage, 126.

Argentina, currency of, 211.

Australia, currency of, 211.

Austria, currency of, 211.

"Available" gold, 148, 149.

B

Balance of trade, 11–14.

Bank of England discount rate, 180, 181, 182.

Belgium, currency of, 211, 212.

Bill of exchange, nature of, 17–19; price of, 23, 24, 25.

Bolivia, currency of, 212.

Brazil, currency of, 212.

British India, currency of, 212.

British Malaya (Straits Settlements), currency of, 213.

Bulgaria, currency of, 213.

C

Cable transfer, 26, 27.

Canada, currency of, 213.

Central Banks, inter-country deposits of, 138; purposes, 139; withdrawal of, 143–145.

Central Bank policy, control of the discount rate, 174–176; public and private rates, 175.

Chile, currency of, 213.

China (Hong Kong), currency of, 214.

China (Shanghai), currency of, 213, 214.

Coin, abrasion, limit of tolerance, 63, 64.

Coin as a medium of international exchange, 68.

Coining of gold in the U. S. A., 59, 60.

Commercial Credits, 117, 118.

Credit element in foreign exchange, 21–25.

Czechoslovakia, currency of, 214.

D

Denmark, currency of, 214.

Depreciated currency, effect on prices, 197; on foreign trade, 199; trade between countries having, 208.

Discount market, effect on exchange, 109, 110.

Discount market at New York, 101, 102; establishment of, 103–108.

Dollar, position in foreign exchange, 82, 83, 104–110.

E

"Earmarked" gold, 145; purpose of earmark, 147, 148.

Equalization Fund, 171, 172.

F

Favorable and unfavorable trade balance, 11, 12, 13.

Federal Reserve Bank, open market operations of, 182–186.